*Scotland in Stamps*

# Scotland in Stamps

A GUIDE TO THE POSTAL HISTORY,
POSTAGE STAMPS AND POSTMARKS
OF SCOTLAND

C. W. HILL

IMPULSE BOOKS  ABERDEEN 1972

First published 1972 by
Impulse Publications Ltd.
28 Guild Street
Aberdeen

BY THE SAME AUTHOR

*Discovering British Postage Stamps*
*Discovering Picture Postcards*

and, for children,

*The Jock and Jonathan Stories*

PRINTED IN GREAT BRITAIN AT
THE UNIVERSITY PRESS
ABERDEEN

*For*

*Janet, who brought me to Scotland,*

*and*

*Jonathan, who came with me*

‿‿‿‿

# *Contents*

## Introduction

This book originated in the author's request at a public library in North-East Scotland for a book about Scottish postage stamps and postal history. After careful search in her bibliography, the librarian replied that there appeared to be no such book in existence. The omission was all the more remarkable because there is so much to be said on the subject.

The purpose of the book, therefore, is to trace the orthodox routes of Scottish philately and to signpost some of the fascinating by-ways which invite further exploration. Everyone, whether artist, historian, economist, transport enthusiast, criminologist or single-minded stamp-collector, is free to follow the path of his choice. That is one of the pleasures of philately.

### ACKNOWLEDGEMENT

The lines from the poem *Night Mail,* by W. H. Auden, are published by permission of the Minister of Posts and Telecommunications.

# 1

## *The Story of the Posts*

In the small, dark hours of Thursday, 24 March 1603 a rider cantered out of the courtyard of the royal palace of Sheen, near Richmond, in Surrey, and turned his horse's head northwards. He had a long journey before him. He carried news which would change the history of two kingdoms, and, through them, of many lands beyond the seas.

The rider was Sir Robert Carey, soldier and courtier. A few hours earlier his Queen, the last Tudor monarch of England, had quietly died, leaving her throne grudgingly to her cousin the King of Scots. This was the news that Sir Robert Carey was speeding north to tell.

Through the dawning and daylight hours he spurred, changing horses every twenty miles or so along the road. By nightfall he reached the post-house at Scrooby, in Nottinghamshire. The next night he rested at Morpeth, in Northumberland, and his journey ended the following evening when he rode into the courtyard of Holyroodhouse, in Edinburgh, to kneel with his news before King James the Sixth of Scotland and First of England, France and Ireland.

Sir Robert's journey of four hundred miles in under three days was not a triumph of hasty improvisation but the result of the efficiency of the Tudor postal service. This had its origins in the need for monarchs to communicate regularly with their officers of state, their local government officials and their ambas-

sadors abroad. Depending on the weather, the condition of the
road and the time of day, it was reckoned that a messenger
carrying despatches could ride about twenty miles before need-
ing a change of horse. The despatch-riders were known as posts
and this word came to be applied also to the points at which
their horses were changed. A postmaster was appointed at each
place – he was usually a local inn-keeper with stabling and
rooms to let – and he was held responsible for the smooth
running of the posts along his section of the road. In overall
charge was a court official known as the Master of the Posts. The
first of whom there is definite record was Sir Brian Tuke, who
was appointed by the English King, Henry VIII about 1510.

Sir Brian's task was not easy. He had occasion to complain
that the postmasters 'many times be fain to take horses out of
the plows and carts, wherein can be no extreme diligence'. As
well as the quality of the horses, overwork was another cause for
complaint. On the Great North Road, said Sir Brian, 'many
times happen two depeches in a day one way, and sometimes
more'. But he persevered with his arrangements and by the time
he died in 1545 the Dover Road and the Great North Road to
Edinburgh had regular posts; private travellers wishing to
journey 'post-haste' were permitted to use the post-houses; and
the post-boys were allowed to carry private letters from courtiers
and state officials. Each postmaster was now enjoined to keep
at least six horses ready in his stables, two for the post-boys and
the others for travellers. This was the service which enabled Sir
Robert Carey to make his momentous journey with tidings for
which the grateful King James appointed him a gentleman of
the bedchamber. He later became chamberlain to the heir to
the throne, the Prince of Wales, and when the Prince was
crowned as King Charles I, Carey was created Earl of
Monmouth.

But the posts were not for ordinary folk. Few people could
read or write and those who could, whether clerics, lairds, law-

yers or merchants, made their own arrangements to send and
receive letters. Friends travelling from place to place, soldiers
going to or returning from the wars, even pedlars and chapmen
might be willing to carry letters. If all else failed a well-to-do
laird or merchant might send his letter by one of his own servants. Enterprising city fathers sometimes appointed a messenger to carry important correspondence. The earliest reference to
a distinctive uniform for postmen, indeed, dates from 1595,
when the Aberdeen magistrates ordered for Alexander Taylor,
'the post', a livery of blue cloth with the armorial bearings of
the town worked in silver thread on his right sleeve. It was
Postie Taylor's job to take the magistrates' despatches to Edinburgh or to any other places where the King held court. The
wealth and importance of trade between Britain and the continent of Europe prompted two classes of merchants to organise
their own regular postal services across the English Channel and
the North Sea. They were the Merchant Adventurers, who were
British merchants with interests abroad, mainly in France and
the Low Countries, and the Merchant Strangers, who were
foreign merchants with establishments in Britain, most of them
being Flemings or Frenchmen centred in London and the
south-east of England. Records of both these private posts are
scanty but they were certainly operating by 1570. Elizabeth I
was so unsure of her throne and her case against Mary Queen
of Scots had relied so strongly on the secret correspondence with
the prisoner's supporters abroad that in 1591 she issued a proclamation forbidding the conveyance of letters or packets into
or out of her kingdom unless the carriers were appointed by her
Master of the Posts.

King James continued Queen Elizabeth's policy of supervising the overseas mails. John Stanhope, who had been Master
of the Posts since 1590, remained in office and was rewarded for
his diligence with a barony. Under him and in direct control
of the foreign mails was a merchant of Flemish origin, Mathew

de Quester. The growing importance of the overseas service was emphasised in 1619, when the King granted De Quester and his son, another Mathew, a patent as 'the first and permanent post-masters of England, for Forraine Parts out of the King's Dom-inions'. There was opposition from the merchants at this strict control of their correspondence and at one stage the Merchant Adventurers went so far as to appoint a rival postmaster of their own. But when Charles I succeeded his father in 1625 he con-firmed the De Questers in their office, taking the view, as his Principal Secretary of State expressed it, that there would be no security for the realm 'if everie man may convey letters under the covers of merchants to whom and what place he pleaseth'. When the time came for a change in the Postmasters for Foreign Parts, however, the King prudently chose two men of whom the Merchant Adventurers approved. One of them, Thomas Witherings, soon became the dominant member of the partnership and proved to be a postal reformer of outstanding ability.

A wealthy London mercer, Witherings had been Harbinger to Queen Henrietta Maria, the French wife of Charles I. In this capacity he had arranged her lodgings when she travelled, so that he had extensive contacts with the continental courts and mail services. Witherings was so successful in his organisation of the posts between London and the continent, via Calais, Dunkirk and Antwerp, that in 1635 the King appointed him to take charge also of the inland posts. The royal proclamation was headed 'For the settling of the letter-office of England and Scotland'.

'Whereas', it began, 'to this time there hath been no certain or constant intercourse between the Kingdoms of England and Scotland, His Majesty hath been graciously pleased to com-mand his servant, Thomas Witherings Esquire, His Majestie's Postmaster of England for foreign parts, to settle a running post or two, to run, night and day, between Edinburgh in Scotland

and the city of London, to go thither and come back again in six days, and to take with them all such letters as shall be directed to any post-town, or any place near any post-town in the said road, which letters to be left at the post-house, or some other house as the said Thomas Witherings shall think convenient; and by-posts to be placed at several places out of the said road, to run and bring in and carry out of the said roads from Lincoln, Hull and other places, as there shall be occasion and answers to be brought again accordingly, and to pay port for the carrying and re-carrying of the said letters . . .'

For single letters from London the rates set out in the Proclamation were:

| | |
|---|---|
| Up to 80 miles | 2d |
| Up to 140 miles | 4d |
| Above 140 miles | 6d |
| To or from Scotland | 8d |
| To or from Ireland | 9d |

Letters containing two sheets of paper were charged double these rates.

The posts were to run along the six principal roads, to Edinburgh, to Dover for the continent, to Chester and Holyhead for Ireland, to Exeter and Plymouth, to Bristol and to Norwich. This regular conveyance of letters along recognised routes at a small fee was the beginning of the modern postal service. Unhappily Witherings was beset by many difficulties, among them the determination of influential merchants in some cities to maintain their unofficial posts, the inefficiency of local postmasters and the jealousy of his partner. Within two years of the momentous Proclamation Witherings was deprived of his position, and his house in 'Sherborne Lane, neere Lumbard Street, in London', ceased to be the hub of the British postal services. Soon the quarrel between King and Parliament brought civil war to the kingdom and chaos to the posts.

The next landmark in postal history came in June 1657, when

Oliver Cromwell, the Lord Protector, gave his assent to 'An Act for the Settling of the Postage of England, Scotland and Ireland'. This was an attempt to re-organise the posts following the defeat of the Royalists and it used for the first time the title of Postmaster-General to designate the official appointed by Parliament to control the postal service. Rates of postage to foreign destinations were listed in detail. A single letter could be sent to Bordeaux or Madrid for 9d and as far as Constantinople for 1s. The office of Postmaster-General was to be farmed out to the highest bidder, whose aim would be to run the posts as cheaply and efficiently as was compatible with the necessity of making a handsome profit for himself. With the restoration in 1660 of King Charles II a new Act was passed to legalise that of 1657 which, in the view of the new government, was an illegal measure passed by a regicidal usurper. But the 1660 Act made no significant changes. The rates of postage, especially within Scotland, were set out in greater detail than in the 1635 Proclamation. They were:

| | |
|---|---|
| Up to 80 miles | 2d |
| Above 80 miles | 3d |
| To or from Berwick | 3d |
| Up to 40 miles from Berwick within Scotland | 2d |
| Above 40 miles from Berwick within Scotland | 4d |
| To Edinburgh | 5d |
| To Dublin | 6d |

The system of farming the office of Postmaster-General was confirmed and a Cavalier colonel, Henry Bishop, of Henfield, Sussex, contracted to pay £21,500 per annum for the privilege of running the posts. Like Witherings, Henry Bishop was an innovator to whom we owe several improvements in the postal services, among them the introduction of date-stamps and slogan postmarks on letters. Like Witherings, too, Bishop did not enjoy a peaceful tenure of office. His successor, another Royalist named Daniel O'Neale, had to contend not only with the normal hazards of running the postal services but with the additional burden placed on the Postmaster-General when King Charles II persuaded Parliament to grant part of the Post Office revenues to his brother the Duke of York, afterwards King James II, and another share to one of his mistresses, the beautiful Barbara Villiers, who later became Lady Castlemaine and Duchess of Cleveland.

Meanwhile the Scottish postal services remained under the handicap of an inadequate road system. Moreover winter snow, spring and autumn rains and summer dust combined to make travelling by such roads as there were a tedious and dangerous undertaking. The Highlands had no regular posts and in 1678 the country's principal post-road, the forty-four miles between Edinburgh and Glasgow, was so badly surfaced that a six-horse coach was taking six days to make the return journey. The news-sheets of the time were full of accounts of highway robberies. On 13 August 1692, for instance, the post-boy riding the last stage to Edinburgh with the English mail was held up by two armed men 'upon the highway from Haddington to Edinburgh, near that place thereof called Jock's Lodge (a mile from town) about ten hours of the night'. The post-boy was relieved not only of his mail but of his horse, too. Since the post-boys usually were literally boys, no more than fifteen or sixteen years of age, they were a constant source of temptation to highwaymen.

Dissatisfaction with the development of the services in Scotland led the Scottish Parliament to pass in 1695 the country's first important legislation 'anent the Post Office'. This established a General Post Office in Edinburgh and fixed the rates of postage for a single letter at 2s (Scottish) to Berwick or within 50 miles of Edinburgh, 3s over 50 miles and 4s over 100 miles. Sir Robert Sinclair, of Stevenson, was appointed Postmaster-General of Scotland with a monopoly of the postal services and an annual salary of £300. Like Henry Bishop in England, Sir

2

Robert found the task arduous and unprofitable, and the following year he relinquished it. The post between London and Edinburgh was now slower than it had been in the time of Thomas Witherings, sixty years before. It had then been planned to take three days for the journey. By the end of the seventeenth century it was taking five days.

After the parliamentary union of Scotland and England in 1707, Queen Anne's ministers decided that 'a correspondence of Posts will be best managed and ordered for the Publick Good by uniting the said two Post Offices under one Postmaster-General'. A less laudable reason for the merger was that money was urgently needed to pay for Britain's long struggle with France, the War of the Spanish Succession. The title of the new act embodied these two features. It was 'An Act for establishing a General Post Office for all Her Majesty's Dominions, and for settling a Weekly Sum of the Revenues thereof, for the service of the War, and other Her Majesty's Occasions'. The immediate result was a rise in postage rates. They now become:

| | |
|---|---|
| Up to 80 miles | 3d |
| Above 80 miles | 4d |
| To Edinburgh | 6d |
| To Dublin | 6d |
| Up to 50 miles from Edinburgh within Scotland | 2d |
| Above 50 miles but not exceeding 80 miles from Edinburgh within Scotland | 3d |
| Above 80 miles from Edinburgh within Scotland | 4d |

Despite the merger, the postmaster of Edinburgh was still dignified by the title of Postmaster-General of Scotland, as an interesting public notice of 1715 shows. Headed 'By Direction of James Anderson, Esquire, Postmaster-General of Scotland', it announces that 'For the Conveniency of the Noblemen and Gentlemen at Stirling, that they may not loose so much as one Post for Correspondence with London, or any Part of that Road, The Post-Master of Stirling is each Tuesday, Thursday and Saturday, commencing on Thursday next the first of December, to send off a Horse Post precisely at Two in the Afternoon, to bring Letters from Stirling to Edinburgh, to answer the Posts which go for England from Edinburgh on Tuesday, Thursday and Saturday Night. The said Horse Post will also carry Letters from Stirling to Edinburgh. And as the Post comes in from London to Edinburgh, there will a Post Horse be sent off with such Letters as are for Stirling. Given at Stirling Tuesday the 29th Day of November, 1715 Years. Ja. Anderson.'

The eighteenth century was a period of rapid expansion in the trade and industry of the United Kingdom. The road system and the postal services shared in this expansion. The work of the road-makers, blind John Metcalf, of Knaresborough, Thomas Telford, of Westerkirk, Dumfries, and John Loudon Macadam, of Ayr, was matched by that of the postal reformers, Ralph Allen, the postmaster of Bath, and John Palmer, a Bath theatre-proprietor.

Ralph Allen's contribution was the organisation of by-posts and cross-posts. By-letters were those which travelled between towns on the same post-road without going as far as London. Because of lack of supervision, dishonest postmasters were able to put into their own pockets a large share of the postage charged on by-letters. Cross-letters were those which travelled between towns on different post-roads but did not go through London. The Post Office lost money on them because even if they were correctly accounted for, the postage on them was less than if the letters were routed through London, since the charges were scaled according to the distance the letter had to travel. Allen persuaded the Post Office to insist on the regular postmarking of letters, introduced by Henry Bishop sixty years earlier, and to call for quarterly returns from all postmasters, giving details of the by-letters and cross-letters they handled. Inspectors, known as surveyors, travelled the roads constantly to ensure that postmasters were obeying the new regulations. The network of posts which Ralph Allen established brought him a fortune. He used much of it in benefactions to the city of Bath, as well as putting aside a thousand pounds each year for private acts of charity. Alexander Pope's couplet provided a fitting epitaph:

> 'Let humble Allen, with an awkward shame,
> Do good by stealth – and blush to find it fame.'

John Palmer, journeying in search of theatrical talent, realised how slowly the post-boys travelled in comparison with the new stage-coaches. He persuaded the Post Office to despatch the mails by coach instead of by 'some idle boy without character, mounted on a worn-out hack'. Not only would the mails be speedier, he urged, but they would also be safer, for the coach could carry a guard 'who is accustomed to the discharge of Fire Arms'. Despite some opposition from the Post Office, John Palmers' proposal was eventually accepted, largely through the influence of the Chancellor of the Exchequer, William Pitt. On 2 August 1784 the first mail-coach, carrying four passengers, the coachman and a guard, left Bristol at four o'clock in the afternoon and arrived in London the next morning at eight. Similar services were rapidly extended to other roads and by 1786 mail-coaches were running regularly and punctually between London and Edinburgh in sixty hours. John Palmer was co-opted to the Post Office to organise the services and by the time he died in 1818 the mail-coach was as picturesque and popular a feature of the British scene as the steam-engine was to be nearly a century later.

Ordinary stage-coaches were painted in a variety of colours but the Royal Mail coaches had a handsome livery of maroon and black, with gleaming brasswork and four well-groomed horses. The guard wore a tall gold-braided hat, scarlet coat and nankeen breeches. He was armed with a blunderbuss, pistols and cutlass, and he carried a long brass post-horn which he blew to warn toll-gate keepers, postmasters and everyone else on the

road of the approach of the Royal Mail. Nineteenth-century
literature abounds in nostalgic references to the mail-coach. De
Quincey's essay on *Going Down with Victory* and a chapter in
Thomas Hughes's *Tom Brown's Schooldays* are among the most
enchanting.

There was a marked contrast between the security of travel by
mail-coach and the hazards faced by travellers away from the
main post-roads. In his book *Memorials of his Time,* published
in 1856, Lord Cockburn, the jurist and Lord Rector of Glasgow
University, described some of the difficulties he had met as a
young advocate depute on circuit. 'Those who are born to
modern travelling', he wrote, 'can scarcely be made to under-
stand how the previous age got on. There was no bridge over the
Tay at Dunkeld, or over the Spey at Fochabers, or over the
Findhorn at Forres. Nothing but wretched, peerless ferries, let
to poor cotters, who rowed, or hauled, or pushed a crazy boat
across, or more commonly got their wives to do it . . . There was
no mail-coach north of Aberdeen till after the battle of
Waterloo.'

Despite their punctuality, their strong construction and the
skill of their drivers, the mail-coaches occasionally met with
mishaps. Broken Bridge, near Elvanfoot, on the Carlisle to Glasgow post-road, owed its name to the collapse of an arch during
a storm on 25 October 1808, which flung the south-bound coach
into the flooded stream below. Two passengers were killed and
the others, with the coachman and guard, had to be rescued by
the coachman and guard of the north-bound coach, which
arrived from Carlisle in the nick of time. Another disaster befell
the mail-coach bound from Dumfries to Edinburgh in a snow-
storm on 1 February 1831. Deep drifts and high winds prevented it from going beyond Moffat but the coachman and guard,
with a local post-boy, hired horses and went on with the
mailbags. Near Erickstane Hill the horses could go no further
so the coachman and guard, after sending the post-boy back

with the horses to Moffat, determined to continue the journey on foot as far as the inn at Tweedshaws, where they hoped to hire fresh horses for the rest of the journey. The bitter cold and driving snow proved too much for them. Their bodies were found five days later in a snowdrift on Erickstane Hill. They had tied the mailbags to a post at the roadside, so ensuring that in spite of their own misfortune, the mail would eventually be recovered.

Passengers boarded the mail-coaches at the inns where the horses were stabled. In London the *Bull and Mouth* in St. Martin's-le-Grand was the terminus for the services to Edinburgh, Aberdeen, Inverness and Glasgow. The coachman then drove to the General Post Office, which was in Lombard Street until 1829 and then in St. Martin's-le-Grand, where the mailbags were loaded for departure at 8 p.m. For each change of horses at the posting inns only two or three minutes were allowed and overall speeds reached ten miles an hour as road surfaces improved. The longest run in the British Isles was from London to Thurso, 783 miles in four days and forty minutes. The timetable in 1836 was:

| | |
|---|---|
| London, the *Bull and Mouth* | 7.30 p.m. |
| General Post Office | 8.00 |
| Waltham Cross | 9.25 |
| Ware | 10.26 |
| Arrington | 12.57 a.m. |
| Huntingdon | 2.30 |
| Stilton | 3.45 |
| Stamford | 5.15 |
| Grantham | 7.25 |
| Newark | 9.30 |
| Barnby Moor | 11.50 |
| Doncaster | 1.12 p.m. |
| Ferrybridge | 2.44 |
| Tadcaster | 3.56 |

| | | |
|---|---|---|
| York | 4.54 | |
| Easingwold | 6.54 | |
| Thirsk | 7.58 | |
| Northallerton | 8.52 | |
| Darlington | 10.28 | |
| Durham | 12.33 | a.m. |
| Newcastle-upon-Tyne | 1.50 | |
| Morpeth | 3.22 | |
| Alnwick | 5.17 | |
| Belford | 6.47 | |
| Berwick-upon-Tweed | 8.17 | |
| Dunbar | 11.41 | |
| Haddington | 12.45 | p.m. |
| Edinburgh arr. | 2.23 | |
| Edinburgh dep. | 4.00 | |
| Kinross | 7.15 | |
| Perth | 9.00 | |
| Dundee | 11.15 | |
| Arbroath | 1.00 | a.m. |
| Montrose | 2.23 | |
| Stonehaven | 4.47 | |
| Aberdeen | 6.22 | |
| Inverurie | 8.54 | |
| Huntly | 11.45 | |
| Keith | 12.58 | |
| Elgin | 3.00 | |
| Nairn | 6.02 | |
| Inverness | 8.06 | |
| Beauly | 12.30 | a.m. |
| Dingwall | 1.30 | |
| Tain | 4.30 | |
| Dornoch | 6.40 | |
| Golspie | 8.20 | |
| Helmsdale | 11.15 | |

| Lybster | 3.20 p.m. |
| Wick | 5.10 |
| Thurso | 8.10 |

Another important service linked London to Portpatrick, where the mail was taken by Post Office sailing-packet and in later years by paddle-steamer to Donaghdee in Northern Ireland. There were two coach routes between Glasgow and Edinburgh but the only service through the Highlands ran from Perth via Kingussie to Inverness. Elsewhere in Scotland the mails went by post-horse or by the letter-carrier on foot.

On 1 May 1830 the *Independent Tally-ho* stage-coach established a record by completing the 109-mile journey from London to Birmingham in a few minutes over seven and a half hours, representing an average speed of more than fourteen miles an hour. Amid the acclaim at this spectacular achievement an event later that year passed almost unnoticed. A single bag of mail was despatched from Liverpool to Manchester by railway train. When the last northbound mail-coach left Newcastle-upon-Tyne for Edinburgh in 1847, flags were flown at half-mast in mourning for the passing of an era.

## Indian Peter's Penny Post

There were some people whom neither King Charles I nor Lord Protector Cromwell could satisfy, at least in postal matters. The rates of postage fixed by the royal proclamation of 1635 and the Act of Parliament of 1657 seem low by modern standards. But the twopence charged on a letter travelling up to eighty miles and the fivepence for a letter from London to Edinburgh were considered expensive in the seventeenth century. A farm labourer's weekly wage of two shillings or a soldier's daily pay of sixpence left little margin for the postage on a letter but it was the literate merchant anxious to expand his business who grumbled most bitterly at the high charges. For nearly two hundred years there was constant agitation for a reduction in postage rates and there were several attempts by enterprising citizens to organise private postal services which could be run more economically than the official service.

In 1659 John Hill, an attorney of York, published a pamphlet in which he attacked the system of farming the Post Office out to the highest bidder. The pamplet was entitled *A Penny Post: or a Vindication of the Liberty and Birthright of every Englishman in carrying Merchants' and other Men's letters, against any restraint of Farmers of such Employment.* In it the author claimed that 'if not restrained by Authority' he would organise the delivery of letters anywhere in England at a postage of one penny, to Scotland for twopence and to Ireland for fourpence.

Nothing more was heard of John Hill after the publication of his pamphlet. He obviously failed in his attack on the Post Office monopoly.

Less ambitious and more successful was a Londoner named William Dockwra. He organised a postal service which, according to a broadsheet he published in April 1680, was to deliver letters and packets 'within the Cities and suburbs of London and Westminster, and all their contiguous buildings . . . and all other places within the Weekly Bills of Mortality, be it farther or nearer'. The expression 'within the weekly bills of mortality' meant in the parishes which made a regular return of the deaths occurring therein. For this service the postage was to be one penny.

Dockwra had several partners in the scheme, one of whom, Robert Murray, later claimed to be its 'inventer', but it was undoubtedly Dockwra's organising ability which made the venture so comprehensive and profitable. He nominated several hundred receiving-houses, most of them taverns, coffee-houses or stationers' shops, where the public could leave letters and packets to be collected by Penny Post messengers and taken to one of seven sorting houses. Deliveries were made at least five times daily in the suburbs and fifteen times a day within the city. A useful feature of the scheme was the introduction of postmarks on the letters. One type, signifying that the postage had been paid, had the words PENNY POST PAID in a triangle, with the initial of the sorting-house, or of the head office in Lime Street, where the letter had been received. The other type of postmark was heart-shaped with the abbreviation 'Mor' for morning or 'Af' for afternoon, followed by a figure signifying the hour at which the letter left the sorting-house for delivery.

Despite some teething troubles, Dockwra's Penny Post soon became so popular that it posed a serious threat to the monopoly of the General Post Office. In 1682 the Postmaster-General brought a legal action against Dockwra, who was fined £100 and ordered to cease operating his Penny Post. But his service had so obviously filled a vital need that within a few weeks it was revived by the Postmaster-General as the London Penny Post and run as a separate concern from the General Post Office until it became the London Twopenny Post in 1801 and was later absorbed into the national postal service. Dockwra himself petitioned for compensation for his efforts on behalf of cheaper postage and he was eventually awarded an annual pension of £500 for ten years.

The next pioneer of private enterprise in the postal service was another Londoner, Charles Povey. For a brief seven months from October 1709 to May 1710, Povey undercut the London Penny Post by organising what he called 'The Halfpenny Carriage.' He modelled this on William Dockwra's Penny Post but instead of so many receiving-houses, he employed messengers 'who rang a Bell every Hour in all Streets, Courts and Lanes', so that 'Persons had the Opportunity to deliver their Letters and small Parcels of Goods at their own Doors, without going into the Cold and Wet to the Receivers Houses, as was before, and is now practised'. The postage on the letters and packets collected by the bell-man was to be only a halfpenny.

For a long time there was no record of Povey's having used postmarks on the mail carried by his service but in 1960 a letter dated January 1710, and bearing a postmark THE HALF-PENNY CARRIAGE in three lines, came to light in the Public Record Office, London. Like Dockwra, Povey was prosecuted for infringing the Post Office monopoly and his service was brought to an abrupt end. A few months later he helped to found an insurance company which became the Sun Life Office and is now the Sun Insurance Company. One feature of Povey's Halfpenny Carriage persisted long after its demise and his death. This was the bell-man, who was adopted by the London Penny Post and later became a familiar figure in the streets of Edinburgh, Glasgow and other British cities. The last bell-man was withdrawn from London streets in 1846 and the introduction of pillar-boxes a few years later made his task unnecessary in other places.

Meanwhile the London Penny Post was now firmly established. Its success led Parliament to pass an Act in 1765 which authorised the General Post Office to introduce local penny posts 'for any City or Town and the Suburbs thereof, and the Places adjacent', where such a service was considered 'necessary and convenient'. The first city to take advantage of this concession was Dublin, where a small and unprofitable penny post began operations in October 1773.

At about the same time a remarkable Scotsman surfaced in Edinburgh. He was Peter Williamson, the story of whose life reads like one of the picaresque novels which were so popular during the eighteenth century and in which the hero moves at incredible speed from mishap to calamity and from calamity to disaster, only to triumph eventually over all adversities, yet leaving the reader certain in the knowledge that the felicity which blossoms at the *Finis* would have lasted no more than another paragraph had the story continued half a page further. It is, indeed, difficult to distinguish fact from fiction in Peter Williamson's story, though Professor Sir Walter Mercer took great pains to do so in an article published in 1961 in the journal of the Postal History Society.

Peter Williamson was born at Aboyne, Aberdeenshire, in 1729. As a child he was sent by his parents to live with an aunt in Aberdeen so that he could attend school there. In those days the trade in African negro slaves was supplemented by a more discreet but profitable enterprise, the kidnapping of young children for trans-shipment to the American plantations, ostensibly as apprentices. One day while playing along the Aberdeen quayside, Peter was decoyed on board a ship by two sailors, who then seized him and clamped him below decks with about fifty other children in the same plight. In his autobiography, *French and Indian Cruelty: the Life and Adventures of Peter Williamson,* there is a graphic account of the hardships suffered by the kidnapped children during the voyage to America. After a rough crossing the ship ran into a gale and was grounded on a sand-bank off Cape May, in Delaware Bay. The captain and crew took to the boats, leaving the children to their fate. It was not until the following morning, when the storm had abated and the sailors returned to the ship to salvage the cargo, that they discovered that the children had also survived.

Peter was then sold in Philadelphia for about £16, his purchaser being a Scottish farmer who had himself been kidnapped as a boy in similar circumstances. The farmer proved a humane master during the seven years that Peter served him. When he died soon afterwards he left Peter £150, his best horse and some of his personal chattels. With the help of this bequest Peter married the daughter of a local farmer and acquired a strip of land on the Delaware River. But he was not allowed to farm his land in peace, for rivalry between French and British settlers led to the French bribing Red Indians to attack British settlements. In one of these attacks Peter's wife was murdered, his farm was burnt and he was carried off as a prisoner. His autobiography describes the tortures inflicted by the Red Indians on other British prisoners and tells of the treatment he himself had to endure. Eventually Peter succeeded in escaping from captivity and he then enlisted in the army to fight the French and their Red Indian allies. Wounded in the hand, he was captured again at Fort George in 1756 and imprisoned in Quebec. Finally he was released and returned to England, landing at Plymouth with six shillings in his pocket.

On his way north, Peter arrived penniless in York, where he gained the sympathy of a local gentleman who read the account the wandering Scotsman had written of his adventures and 'thought it proper to have it printed for his benefit and cheerfully subscribed to this end'. By selling copies of this short autobiography and by putting on Red Indian dress and demonstrating war-whoops, Peter was able to complete his journey. On arrival in Aberdeen, however, he fell foul of the city fathers by accusing one of their number, Bailie William Fordyce, of being responsible for his kidnapping and that of other young Aberdonians. Peter was arrested, forced to withdraw the accusation, fined ten shillings and turned out of the city as a vagrant.

Peter, now nicknamed 'Indian Peter' because of his adventures in North America and his spectacular impersonations of a Red Indian on the warpath, made his way to Edinburgh, where he opened a tavern, known as *Indian Peter's Coffee House,* in the hall of the Parliament House. He found time also to take action in the Court of Session against the corporation of Aberdeen and was awarded £100 damages and his costs. His next move was to an inn, which he named *Peter's Tavern,* in Old Parliament Close, and this proved so profitable that he was able to open a bookshop and printing-house in the Luckenbooths, on the north side of St. Giles's Cathedral. It was here that in 1773 he printed the first *Edinburgh Directory.* In the second edition of this, dated May 1774, Peter made an historic announcement. 'The Publisher', it read, 'takes this opportunity to acquaint the Public that he will always make it his study to dispatch all letters and parcels, not exceeding three pounds in weight, to any place within an English mile to the East, South and West of the Cross of Edinburgh, and so far as South and North Leith, every hour through the day, for one penny each letter or bundle.' Among the receiving-agents who accepted letters and parcels for the Edinburgh Penny Post were:

Peter Williamson, at his printing-house in Swan's Close.

James Grant, grocer, head of Halkerston's Wynd.

William Lockhart, shoemaker, third door within the Cowgate Head.

John Rae, merchant, at the sign of the Roebuck, Grassmarket.

William Ronald, merchant, corner shop, Tolbooth Wynd, Leith.

George Maitland, vintner, on the shore of Leith.

The letter-carriers, called caddies, wore hats with the words 'Penny Post' on them and letters were postmarked to show whether the postage had been prepaid by the sender or was to be collected on delivery to the addressee. The postmarks take several forms, one being in a straight line, 'EDIN Dec 22d. 1773. 1d' and others being circular. The latter read 'PENNY POST PAID' or 'E. PENNY POST NOT PAID', sometimes with the date in the centre. The postmarks were struck in black or red ink, the latter being scarcer.

Although Peter Williamson's Edinburgh Penny Post was a private venture, he was more fortunate than William Dockwra and Charles Povey, for he was allowed to operate it until July 1793. A visit to Edinburgh by a Post Office surveyor, Francis Freeling, led to the decision to absorb the Penny Post into the Edinburgh General Post Office. Freeling recommended that a pension of £25 a year should be paid to Peter Williamson in compensation for the loss of his undertaking. The Treasury concurred and the pension was paid until his death on 19 January 1799.

Following the take-over by the General Post Office, the Edinburgh Penny Post was slowly expanded. By the 1830's the service covered an area extending from Cramond and Newhaven in the north to Penicuik and Ford in the south, and from Prestonpans and Tranent in the east to Uphall and Winchburgh, then known as Wenchbro, in the west. Many new postmarks were introduced, some circular and others oval or rectangular. They signified the receiving-house where the letter had been posted, the time it had been handed in, and whether the postage had been prepaid or not. Typical postmarks read P.P. Pd., LIBERTON PENNY POST, DUKE STREET P.P.O., PENNYCUICK P.P.O. UNPAID, and PENNY POST – 8 MORNING – UN-

PAID. Clearly struck examples, especially of the earlier postmarks, are scarce. An instruction issued to all Scottish postmasters in December 1807 offers a clue to this scarcity. 'Stamp
all letters that are to be forwarded from your office with wooden
stamp,' it read, 'using common writing ink for the purpose of
making the impression. On no account whatever apply the
smoke of candle for the purpose; should you do so the whole
letter will be completely destroyed.'

During 1793, while Peter Williamson's Penny Post was being
taken over by the General Post Office, local penny posts were
being established in Manchester, Bristol and Birmingham,
The Glasgow Penny Post followed a few years later, in 1800,
although the revenue raised during its first year of operation was
less than £100, indicating that on average fewer than eighty
letters were posted daily in Glasgow for local delivery. By 1840
there were penny posts in about a hundred Scottish towns, en-
compassing over four hundred suburbs and villages, some of
them as much as twenty miles from the town centre. The Banff
Penny Post, for instance, had offices at Cornhill, Macduff and
Rothiemay; the Perth Penny Post had offices at Bankfoot,
Methuen, Scone and Stanley; and the Stirling Penny Post ran
to offices at Alva, Bannockburn, Blairlogie, Bridge of Allan,
Menstrie, Port of Menteith, St. Ninian's and Thornhill.

In his book *The Royal Mail: its Curiosities and Romance*,
published by William Blackwood and Sons in 1884, James
Wilson Hyde, who was Superintendent in the Edinburgh General Post Office, described the introduction of a local post in the
wilds of Perthshire. This was about 1800 when the Post Office
'had not as yet carried its civilising influence into the districts
of Balquhidder, Lochearnhead, Killin and Tyndrum'. The
annual cost of providing the service was:

A runner to travel from Callander to Lochearnhead – fourteen miles – at 2s a journey, three
   times a week                                    £15  12  0

| | | | |
|---|---|---|---|
| Salary to postmaster of Lochearnhead | 5 | 0 | 0 |
| A runner from Lochearnhead to Killin – eight miles – at 1s a journey, three times a week | 7 | 16 | 0 |
| Salary to postmaster of Killin | 5 | 0 | 0 |
| Receiving-house at Wester Lix | 2 | 0 | 0 |
| Runner thence to Luib – four or five miles – 1s 6d per week | 3 | 18 | 0 |
| Office at Luib | 4 | 0 | 0 |
| Total | £43 | 6 | 0 |

'It may be proper, however,' added Superintendent Hyde, 'to remark in this connection that money then was of greater value than now.' But even allowing for the changes in the value of money, the local posts of the early nineteenth century were comparatively cheap, rapid and efficient. It was the long distance services which were expensive, slow and inefficient. A Greenock Member of Parliament played a vital part in the campaign launched by a Worcestershire ex-schoolmaster named Rowland Hill to put an end to this disparity.

### 3

## *Letters for a Penny*

Among the new members elected to Parliament as a result of the Reform Acts of 1832 was Greenock's first M.P., Robert Wallace. Born in 1773 the son of a wealthy West India merchant of Kelly, Ayrshire, Wallace soon made his mark in the House by his probing questions about postal affairs. 'I never take up my papers in the morning', complained Lord William Lennox, 'that I do not find the hon. member for Greenock there with some motion for inquiry with respect to the Post Office.'

Robert Wallace queried the salary paid to the formidable Sir Francis Freeling, Secretary of the Post Office for almost forty years. He accused the Postmaster-General, the Duke of Richmond, of being 'guilty of a felony in the opening of letters' during the investigation of a case of fraud. He proposed that the contract for the construction of mail-coaches should be awarded by open tender instead of being the monopoly of a London coach-builder. He advocated the use of steamships for carrying the mails between Glasgow and the West of Scotland. But it was against the high cost of sending or receiving a letter that Robert Wallace made his sharpest attacks. He had good cause for complaint. A letter from London to Greenock cost 1s $2\frac{1}{2}$d and one from Glasgow to Greenock cost 6d. Yet there were places, such as Balfron, which were further from Glasgow than Greenock but to which letters could be sent for one penny because they lay within the area covered by the Glasgow Penny Post.

High as it was, the postage on a letter was doubled if the letter
contained two sheets of paper and trebled if it contained three.
Since an envelope was reckoned as an extra sheet, people seldom
used envelopes, preferring to fold the letter, seal it with wax or
an adhesive wafer and write the name and address of the
addressee on the outside. Post Office clerks had to examine each
letter against the light of a candle to determine how many
sheets of paper it contained. This practice was a temptation to
dishonesty. An Edinburgh advocate depute, G. Napier, related
to Rowland Hill the story of a theft which illustrated the risk
involved. In January 1834, Mr. Duncan, a Liverpool merchant,
addressed a letter containing a Bank of England £50 note to his
mother at Broughty Ferry. The old lady was expecting the letter
and when it did not arrive she wrote to tell her son, who immediately informed the Bank. No trace of the letter could be found
at the post offices through which it should have passed, those
at Liverpool, Edinburgh, Dundee and Broughty Ferry. Meanwhile one of the tellers at the Commercial Bank in Edinburgh,
visiting a theatre, happened to notice particularly the man in
the seat in front of him. The following day he was surprised to
see the same man, muffled in a cloak, with a fur cap pulled low
over his forehead and wearing green spectacles, presenting to
another teller in the Commercial Bank a £50 Bank of England
note, asking for it to be changed for Commercial Bank notes.
The stranger wrote his name as 'Jo. Wilford, College Post Office'
on the back of the £50 note before departing with his change.

Out of mere curiosity the teller who had noticed the stranger
in the theatre and again in his Bank asked his colleague who
the man might be, and was shown the name on the back of the
banknote. A few days later the banknote was returned from the
Bank of England as having been stolen from the letter posted
in Liverpool by Mr. Duncan. With the slender clue of the fic-
titious name and address on the back of the note, the teller was
asked to go to the Edinburgh Post Office to watch the clerks

arriving for duty. Among them he recognised the stranger, who proved to be a James W. Nicol. The fur cap and green spectacles were found at his lodgings and the cloak, enquiries revealed, had been borrowed. Nicol was charged with the theft and pleaded guilty. He had yielded to sudden temptation when holding the Liverpool letter up to a light to determine whether it contained one or two sheets of paper, so that the rate of post-age could be confirmed. Nicol's punishment for stealing the fifty pounds was transportation for life. For Rowland Hill the moral of this cautionary tale was that if the postage had not been so excessive, the banknote would have been cut into two pieces to be sent in separate letters and if the postage had been calculated according to the weight of the letter, there would have been no need for the post office clerk to examine its contents against a strong light and thus fall into temptation.

The excessive rates of postage, moreover, were a serious handicap to trade and a heavy burden on the poor. They brought little benefit to the Post Office, for despite a steady increase in the population of the United Kingdom between 1815 and 1835, there was a decrease in the annual revenue from the postal services. Whenever possible, people avoided sending their letters by post and used instead the services provided by carriers or private travellers. One Glasgow publisher and bookseller, John Reid, admitted sending and receiving about fifty letters or circulars daily. 'I was not caught', he admitted, 'till I had sent twenty thousand letters, etc., otherwise than through the post.' Growing support for Robert Wallace's campaign to end such abuses by reforming the Post Office service came from all parts of the United Kingdom and from all sections of the community but above all from Rowland Hill.

Born in 1795 at Kidderminster, where his father owned a private school, Rowland Hill was one of eight children, all of them talented. The family moved to Wolverhampton and then to Birmingham, finally opening a school in an old mansion,

Bruce Castle, at Tottenham. Rowland Hill taught there for a time but also busied himself with the study of astronomy, a project for the education of pauper children and the invention of a newspaper-printing machine. In 1835 he became secretary to the South Australian Colonisation Commission and at the same time turned his attention to the subject of Post Office reform. He soon made the acquaintance of Robert Wallace who on one occasion sent him a cab-load of books, reports and minutes concerning Post Office affairs. Armed with such material Rowland Hill published in January 1837 the first edition of an historic pamphlet, *Post Office Reform; Its Importance and Practicability.* In this he set out his arguments, supporting them by statistics drawn from official sources. The most remarkable was his calculation of the cost of conveying a letter from London to Edinburgh, a service for which the Post Office charged 1s 1½d.

ESTIMATE OF THE COST OF CONVEYING A LETTER FROM LONDON
TO EDINBURGH, A DISTANCE OF 400 MILES

## MILEAGE ON THE WHOLE MAIL

|  | £ | s. | d. |
|---|---|---|---|
| From London to York, 196 miles, at 1 9/16d. per mile | 1 | 5 | 6¼ |
| From York to Edinburgh, 204 miles, at 1½d. per mile | 1 | 5 | 0 |
|  | 2 | 10 | 6¼ |
| Guards' Wages – Say six Guards, one day each, at 10s 6d per week | 0 | 10 | 6 |
| Allow for Tolls (which are paid in Scotland) and all other expenses | 1 | 18 | 11¾ |
| Total cost of conveying the Mail once from London to Edinburgh, including the Mails of all intermediate places | 5 | 0 | 0 |

The average weight of the mail conveyed by the London and Edinburgh mail coach is about    8 cwt.

Deduct for the weight of the bags, say       2

----

Average weight of letters, newspapers, etc.     6

The cost of conveyance is therefore per cwt.        16s 8d

Per ounce and a half, the average weight of a newspaper, about
    one-sixth of a penny.

Per quarter of an ounce, the average weight of a single letter,
    about one thirty-sixth of a penny.

Basing his argument upon this calculation, Rowland Hill
advocated that letters weighing up to half an ounce should be
delivered anywhere within the United Kingdom for one penny,
with another penny for each additional half ounce. To save
time in delivery he proposed that postage should be prepaid
instead of being collected by the postman from the addressee,
as had previously been the usual practice. In the second edition
of the pamphlet he amplified this proposal of prepayment by
suggesting the introduction of stamped letter-sheets and envelopes so that letters need not be handed over the post office
counter but could be posted in letter-boxes. There was one difficulty which these letter-sheets and envelopes would not overcome. An illiterate person, such as a servant, bringing a letter
to be posted might not be able to address the envelope he purchased. So, proposed Hill, the Post Office should also sell for
one penny 'a bit of paper just large enough to bear the stamp,
and covered at the back with a glutinous wash, which the
bringer might, by applying a little moisture, attach to the back
of a letter'. This proposal was the genesis of the adhesive postage
stamp.

In official circles Hill's pamphlet was coolly received. The
Postmaster-General, the Earl of Lichfield, said that of 'all the
wild and visionary schemes which he had ever heard or read of,
it was the most extravagant'. But public opinion was overwhel-
mingly in Hill's favour. Meetings were organised in support of
his scheme for uniform penny postage, newspapers campaigned

in favour of it and Members of Parliament were begged by their constituents to speak for it. Eventually, through the persistence of Robert Wallace, the government agreed to appoint a Select Committee 'to inquire into the present rates or modes of charging postage, with a view to such reduction thereof as may be made without injury to the revenue; and for this purpose, to examine especially into the mode recommended, of charging and collecting postage, in a pamphlet by Mr. Rowland Hill'.

Wallace's part in the campaign was recognised by his appointment as chairman of the committee. Even then the path to reform was far from smooth. Only by the casting vote of the chairman was the proposal for a uniform rate of postage agreed upon and despite the chairman's pleas the proposal for a rate of one penny was rejected in favour of a rate of twopence per half ounce. The committee did, however, agree to recommend the abolition of the franking privilege by which Members of Parliament, Peers and officers of state were allowed to send their mail free of charge simply by signing their names on the cover and adding the date and place of posting. Meanwhile public agitation in favour of the uniform penny post continued. Rowland Hill published more pamphlets, more petitions were addressed to Parliament, Queen Victoria was rumoured to favour the measure and eventually even the Duke of Wellington gave way. The Postal Duties Bill was introduced in Parliament and on 17 August 1839 received the Royal Assent.

The limelight was now turned on Rowland Hill but he always acknowledged his debt to Robert Wallace, while Wallace was equally generous in his praise of Hill. In 1846, following financial difficulties which forced him to sell some of his West Indian property, Wallace resigned from Parliament. Three years later Rowland Hill helped to organise a subscription among his friends on behalf of the Scottish reformer and this enabled Wallace to spend his remaining years in comparative comfort at his home, Seafield, in Greenock. He died there on 1 April 1855.

As soon as the Postal Duties Act had become law, the Treasury announced a competition in which 'artists, men of science and the public in general' were invited to submit suggestions as to the best method of introducing the proposed new postage stamps. A prize of £200 was offered for the best suggestion and one of £100 for the runner-up. Over 2,600 suggestions were received, of which about fifty envisaged small adhesive postage stamps, many of the others preferring stamped wrappers or covers. None of the entries was entirely satisfactory but payments of £100 each were made for the four considered most useful. One of these went to Benjamin Cheverton, of Camden Town, whose suggestion almost certainly influenced the Treasury in the choice of a design for the first postage stamps. Cheverton suggested that the stamps should bear 'a female head of the greatest beauty' because a portrait would be difficult for would-be forgers to copy exactly. 'It so happens,' he wrote, 'that the eye being educated to the perception of differences in the features of the face, the detection of any deviation in the forgery would be more easy – the difference of *effect* would strike an observer more readily than in the case of letters or any mere mechanical or ornamental device, although he may be unable, perhaps, to point out where the difference lies, or in what it consists.'

One of the Treasury's constant fears was that unscrupulous printers would produce forgeries of the new stamps and Cheverton's proposal offered an obvious deterrent. The choice fell upon a profile portrait of the young Queen Victoria by William Wyon, R.A., chief engraver at the Royal Mint. The portrait had formed the obverse design of medallions struck to commemorate the Queen's first official visit to the Corporation of London in November 1837. From the medallion portait Henry Corbould, F.S.A., made water-colour sketches and these were used by two engravers, Charles Heath and his son Frederick, as models for engraving the printing-die for the printers, Perkins, Bacon and

Petch, of Fleet Street, London. Two values were prepared, a One Penny Black for use on letters weighing up to half an ounce and a Twopenny Blue for overweight letters.

The printers met with several difficulties during production of the stamps, particularly in the gumming of the sheets, and when uniform penny postage was introduced on 10 January 1840, the stamps were still not ready. By mid-April the difficulties had been overcome and specimens of the Penny Black were sent to all postmasters, with instructions as to the post-marking of the stamps and measures to be taken if any forgeries were suspected. On 1 May the Penny Black stamps were placed on sale in London, the Twopenny Blues following a day or two later. Wednesday, 6 May 1840 was the day when the stamps were to be used for the first time. Examples are known of Penny Blacks having been used before the official first day but one of the most spectacular discoveries was made in 1968 by Mr. W. G. Morris, president of the Kircudbright Philatelic Society. It was a letter addressed to Mr. James Birnie, of Kircudbright, bearing ten Penny Blacks and posted on their first day of use, 6 May 1840. The high rate of postage had been due to the enclosure of heavy legal documents. When sold at the London auction-rooms of H. R. Harmer Ltd., on 27 May 1968, the letter-sheet realised £4,800.

Over sixty million Penny Blacks were printed and many have survived, mainly because envelopes were not in general use in 1840 so that lawyers, lovers and others who kept their letters also preserved the stamps on the outside of them. In 1900 stamp dealers were offering used specimens of the Penny Black at sixpence each and by 1940 the price had risen to five shillings but with the steady increase in the popularity of philately, the Penny Black has also become much more expensive, as almost every philatelist likes to have an example of the world's first adhesive postage stamp in his collection. Fewer of the Twopenny Blue stamps were issued, so that these have always been more valuable than the Penny Blacks. In 1946 Mr. Alexander Martin, secretary of the Duke of Buccleuch, discovered a block of forty-eight unused Twopenny Blue stamps in an old leather writing-case in the library at Dalkeith Palace, the ducal seat. The stamps, which had lain undisturbed for over a century, realised £6,300 when sold in June 1946, also by H. R. Harmer Ltd.

Among the unsuccessful entries in the Treasury competition for suggestions for the new postage stamps was one from a Dundee bookseller and publisher named James Chalmers. He sent specimens of circular stamps about 1¼ ins. in diameter and printed in black or red. They were inscribed 'General Postage – One Penny' round the edge and, in the centre, 'Not ex. half an oz.' There were similar designs for twopenny stamps and specimens of suggested postmarks reading 'USED – DUNDEE Oct. 7, 39' were printed across the stamps. In his covering letter Chalmers wrote: 'I take the liberty of submitting to your Lordships the details of a plan which, so far back as December, 1837, I announced to Mr. Wallace, M.P., the chairman of the Postage Committee, which was published in the *Post Circular* of 5th April, 1838, and which I have now more fully matured.' He went on to point out the merits of his proposal. The stamps could easily be affixed to a letter, they would not add to its bulk or weight, they would be cheap to produce and they would be convenient to carry. The proposal was accompanied by a testimonial signed by a number of prominent Dundonians but it was not among the prize-winners in the competition. This caused considerable disappointment in Dundee, where Chalmers was well known as a supporter of liberal causes, among them parliamentary reform, the emancipation of the negro slaves and the improvement of the postal services.

The original specimen stamps which Chalmers had sent to Robert Wallace, M.P., on 4 December 1837 had differed from those accompanying his entry in the Treasury competition.

They had measured about one inch square and were inscribed, within an ornamental border, 'General Postage – NOT EXCEEDING HALF AN OUNCE – One Penny'. Two months later Chalmers printed more specimans of these stamps and published leaflets setting out his arguments in their favour. These publications formed the basis for a bitter controversy which began more than twenty-five years after his death in 1853 between his son Patrick and Sir Rowland Hill's son Pearson. James himself appears to have acknowledged that Rowland Hill had the prior right to be regarded as the inventor of adhesive postage stamps but in 1879, the year of Sir Rowland Hill's death, Patrick Chalmers began a long campaign for the recognition of his father as their originator. Pearson Hill replied courteously at first but as letters and pamphlets proliferated both men became more strident and irritable. Patrick, who was living in Wimbledon, wrote of Pearson's 'incoherent attempts to disparage the work of James Chalmers' while Pearson ended a pamphlet in 1888 with the observation that 'surely if the Commissioners in Lunacy are in want of a promising case they might find one at Wimbledon admirably adapted to their hands.' Even as late as 1940 Chalmer's grand-daughter Leah and Colonel H. W. Hill, a grandson of Rowland Hill, were still disputing the question.

The Chalmers case has been refurbished and well presented in *James Chalmers, Inventor of the Adhesive Postage Stamp* by W. J. Smith and J. E. Metcalfe, published in 1970 by David Winter and Son Ltd. But there is probably no last word to be said in the matter. Small adhesive labels bearing the royal cypher had been printed by the Stamp Office since the early eighteenth century for the purpose of collecting the revenue on such items as patent medicines, hats and wig-powder, so that such a concept was not entirely new. Sir Rowland Hill, as witness his generous references to the work of Robert Wallace, was not reluctant to give credit where he believed it was due and there is a strong possibility that Hill and Chalmers arrived independently at the same conclusion.

In any event, Rowland Hill did not foresee the important part which the small adhesive stamp came to play in his scheme of uniform penny postage. He had pinned his faith rather in the provision of penny and twopenny stamped covers and letter-sheets, which seemed to him more convenient, except for the illiterate. Placed on sale in May 1840, with the postage stamps, these covers and letter-sheets had an allegorical design by a well-known Irish-born artist, William Mulready, R.A. The design filled the top and sides of the front of the cover, leaving a space at the bottom for the addressee's name and address. It showed Britannia and the British Lion seated on a rocky islet, despatching messengers to left and right, their destinations being symbolised by Arabs with camels, Indians on elephants, Chinese mandarins, Quakers, Red Indians and other rapturous recipients. But the design struck a false note and the 'Mulreadys', as they came to be called, were greeted with derision. One journal explained the allegory in verses beginning:

'Britannia is sending her messengers forth
To the east, to the west, to the south, to the north;
At her feet is a lion wot's taking a nap
And a dish-cover rests on her legs and her lap.
To the left is a Mussulman writing a letter –
His knees form a desk for want of a better.'

There was caustic comment, too, when one of Britannia's messengers was seen to have only one leg.

Enterprising printers caught the public mood and quickly produced imitations of the Mulreadys in satirical designs. In some of these Britannia is replaced by the Lord Mayor of London, flanked by Gog and Magog with the city coat-of-arms below, or by Pantaloon carving a large Christmas pudding while Harlequin, Columbine, the Punch-and-Judy men and other seasonal characters are featured in vignettes at the sides. An

Edinburgh printer, A. Menzies, of Princes Street, published a caricature showing Britannia as a washer-woman. The Mulreadys were so vigorously lampooned that sales of them were seriously affected. They were replaced within a year by envelopes bearing a small imprinted stamp with an embossed portrait of Queen Victoria and about twenty years later the unsold Mulreadys were officially burned. One unexpected effect of the ill-fated Mulreadys and their caricatures was to popularise pictorial envelopes, some of which were humorous, others sentimental or patriotic. Later came envelopes designed to support campaigns for causes such as international peace, temperance, the abolition of negro slavery in the United States and the reduction of international rates of postage. James Valentine, of Dundee, himself an active social reformer, designed and printed many of these propaganda envelopes and examples of his art are much prized by collectors. Particularly interesting are the Valentine envelopes which advocated cheaper international postage with such slogans as 'Britain from Thee the World expects an Ocean Penny Postage to make her Children one Fraternity'. Uniform cheap postage was a boon which Victorian Britain was happy to export, so that the whole world, or at least those parts of it coloured red in the atlases, should be able to send 'letters for a penny'.

## Scotland's Own Stamps

'Haggis on Scots stamps?' asked a writer in the *Yorkshire Observer* in 1956. 'How does one produce an artistic study of a haggis?' The questions were prompted by an announcement made by the Postmaster-General, Dr. Charles Hill, in the House of Commons on 18 July 1956. In reply to a question from a Welsh M.P., Dr. Hill said: 'Her Majesty the Queen has graciously approved in principle the issue of new stamps in the 2½d, 4d and 1s 3d denominations for Scotland, Wales and Northern Ireland, and a 2½d stamp in Jersey, Guernsey and the Isle of Man. The basic design of the stamps will remain unchanged. The Head of Her Majesty will continue to be the dominant feature. The border will bear symbols or designs appropriate to the places I have mentioned. I propose to invite committees representative of cultural interests in these areas to advise on detailed designs for me to submit to Her Majesty for approval. The new stamps will be on sale only in the areas which they represent, but they will be valid for postage and revenue purposes throughout the British Isles.'

Despite opposition from some conservative philatelists, who expressed the opinion that the new stamps were intended to tempt more money from collectors' pockets, the Postmaster-General's announcement had a favourable though unenthusiastic reception. 'Serious philatelists will probably criticise the project to have separate stamps,' said the *Glasgow Herald,* 'but it is probably sufficient answer for anyone else just to say "Why not?" Pictorials are still banned . . . following the stern tradition that, for this country, the Sovereign's head is identification sufficient of the place of origin, and the distinctiveness will be confined to representation of national or local emblems. Except for this minor alteration in design the stamps will remain virtually identical, and the philatelist in Outer Mongolia – they exist there, too – may have some difficulty in deciding which is a leopard and which is a lion, and which is a rose and which is a thistle.' The general opinion was summed up by *The Scotsman*. 'The announcement . . . is not likely to set the heather on fire but it is a pleasant thought that some particularly Scottish device will wing its way on letters and postcards round the world.'

The decision to allow Scotland and other constituent members of the United Kingdom, except England itself, to have their own distinctive stamps came at the end of a long campaign. When the Penny Blacks were being prepared in 1840 the name 'Great Britain' was not included in the design because the stamps were intended only for internal use and the Queen's portrait was deemed sufficient identification. As other countries began to copy the British scheme of uniform cheap postage, some put their names on their stamps but others, among them Brazil (1843), Belgium (1849), Luxembourg (1852) and the Netherlands (1852), did not. With the formation of the Universal Postal Union to regulate the inter-change of mail among the countries of the world, members were asked to inscribe their names, in Latin characters as far as possible, on their stamps but this invitation is still occasionally ignored by some countries while Britain, by tacit agreement, has been allowed to ignore it entirely. The other main feature of the Penny Black, the choice of the ruling monarch's portrait as the dominant motif of the design, has also hardened into tradition. Several attempts were made after the Second World War to persuade the Post Office to issue pictorial stamps as so many other countries were doing but all attempts foundered on the firm resolve to retain the monarch's portrait.

One of the most persistent advocates of pictorial stamps was a Scottish peer, Viscount Elibank, who was an expert philatelist. Opening a debate in the House of Lords on 17 May 1956, Lord Elibank asked whether the government would consider issuing small pictorial stamps of low face value, bearing the monarch's head but also depicting some of the scenic beauties and historic buildings of the British Isles. Such stamps, he argued, would assist the British Travel and Holidays Association and the Scottish Tourist Board in attracting holidaymakers to the United Kingdom. In support of his proposal Lord Elibank showed a series of seven designs prepared by Charles P. Rang, editor of *Gibbons Stamp Monthly*, featuring a small portrait of the Queen with typical British scenes, among them a distant view of Edinburgh Castle and a Highland loch. Lord Macpherson of Drumochter, also a philatelist, and Lord Geddes were among the speakers who agreed with Lord Elibank but Lord Chesham, replying to the debate, was non-committal though he did say that 'the Postmaster-General has been giving a good deal of thought to the whole question of stamp policy and his mind is by no means closed to such suggestions as have been put forward'.

This debate over stamp design had centred on the small low-value definitive stamps for ordinary use. Commemorative stamps, beginning with the first, issued to mark the opening of the British Empire Exhibition at Wembley in April 1924, were usually larger than the low-value definitives and this gave designers scope to add symbols appropriate to the occasion being commemorated, such as the five linked circles on the Olympic Games series of 1948 or, on the 1951 high values of King George VI, St. George and the Dragon, H.M.S. *Victory* and a view of the white cliffs of Dover. The first 10s stamp of Queen Elizabeth

II, issued on 1 September 1955, had a view of Edinburgh Castle, other values showing the castles of Carrickfergus (2s 6d), Caernarvon (5s) and Windsor (£1). But Dr. Charles Hill's announcement of the small 'regional' issues, as they came to be called, represented a radical change in British stamp-issuing policy.

On 1 October 1957, while the new designs were being prepared, there was a rise in postal rates so that when the stamps were placed on sale the following year they were in values of 3d (the 1-ounce inland letter rate), 6d (the 1-ounce foreign letter rate) and 1s 3d (a ½-ounce overseas airmail letter rate). On 17 May 1965 another rise in postage rates brought a need for a 4d stamp (the 2-ounce inland letter rate) and on 3 October 1966 a further rise led to the need for a 9d stamp (for 1-ounce letters going to foreign destinations by sea) and a 1s 6d stamp (for ½-ounce airmail letters going to certain overseas destinations). All these needs were met by the issue of new 4d, 9d and 1s 6d values in the regional series for Scotland, Northern Ireland, and Wales and Monmouthshire, but only of new 4d stamps in the three islands, which continued to use ordinary British stamps on their foreign-bound mail.

Yet another increase in postal rates on 16 September 1968 brought the postage on inland letters going by first class mail to 5d. As the Post Office intended to use royal blue for all the 5d stamps prepaying this rate, the blue 4d stamps were replaced on 4 September 1968 by 4d stamps in sepia for use on second class inland mail. Unfortunately post office sorters working in artificial light had difficulty in distinguishing between the royal blue 5d stamps and the sepia 4d stamps, so that yet another change had to be made. On 26 February 1969 the sepia 4d stamps were replaced by 4d stamps in vermilion. All these later regional stamps were in the same basic designs as the original three. The 3d, 4d and 5d stamps, designed by Gordon F. Huntly, showed the Queen's portrait flanked by two traditional Scottish emblems, the Crowned Thistle and the Saltire, or St.

4

Andrew's Cross, encircled by a Crown. The 6d and 9d stamps, designed by J. B. Fleming, showed the Queen's portrait in an oval frame flanked by stylised thistles. On the 1s 3d and 1s 6d stamps, designed by A. B. Imrie, two unicorns flanked the Queen's portrait, one supporting a flag bearing the Lion Rampant of Scotland and the other supporting a flag bearing St. Andrew's Cross. The basic list of these Scottish regional issues was:

| | |
|---|---|
| 3d lilac | issued 18 August 1958 |
| 6d purple | 29 September 1958 |
| 1s 3d green | 29 September 1958 |
| 4d blue | 7 February 1966 |
| 9d green | 1 March 1967 |
| 1s 6d greyish-blue | 1 March 1967 |
| 4d sepia | 4 September 1968 |
| 5d royal blue | 4 September 1968 |
| 4d vermilion | 26 February 1969 |

This simplified series is usually extended by specialist collectors to include the issues which had transparent lines of phosphor ink on their faces. These stamps were issued in connection with Post Office experiments with electronic letter-facing machines, the first of which was installed at the Southampton head office in December 1957. The early experiments were made with stamps having black graphite lines on their backs but further experience showed that the lines of phosphor ink were a more satisfactory means of activating the letter-facing machinery. Two printing processes, photogravure and typography, were used for applying the lines to the stamps and specialists can also identify three types of phosphor ink according to the colour, green, blue or violet, which they emit under an ultra-violet lamp. In addition there have been instances of misplaced or missing phosphor lines but these are of interest only to the most dedicated philatelist. The phosphor lines are best seen by holding the stamp horizontal at eye level and letting the light glance along it so that the phosphor appears as one or two dull bars running from top to bottom of the design. Stamps intended for use mainly on printed matter or second class mail were overprinted with one phosphor line and as changes in rates of postage were made, the number of lines had to be adjusted. The introduction of a new type of dull gum, polyvinyl alcohol, known to philatelists as PVA, instead of the traditional shiny gum arabic, provided a minor variety in the regional stamps. The discontinuance of watermarks in the paper on which the stamps were printed after November 1967 provided yet another variety. The complete Scottish regional series, including the phosphor line and watermark changes, is listed in *The British Commonwealth Stamp Catalogue* published by Stanley Gibbons Ltd. and a much more detailed study, including minor printing flaws, is made in the same publishers' *Great Britain Specialised Stamp Catalogue, Volume 3: Queen Elizabeth II*. The following list gives the main varieties.

*3d lilac*
watermarked paper (overall pattern of small crowns)
(a) plain
(b) two phosphor lines
(c) one phosphor line at side
(d) one phosphor line in centre
unwatermarked paper
(e) one phosphor line in centre, gum arabic
(f) one phosphor line in centre, PVA gum
*4d blue*
watermarked paper
(a) plain
(b) two phosphor lines
unwatermarked paper
(c) two phosphor lines, gum arabic
(d) two phosphor lines, PVA gum
*4d sepia*

(a) unwatermarked, one phosphor line in centre, PVA gum
*4d vermilion*
(a) unwatermarked, one phosphor line in centre, PVA gum
*5d royal blue*
(a) unwatermarked, two phosphor lines, PVA gum
*6d purple*
(a) watermarked, plain
(b) watermarked, two phosphor lines
*9d green*
(a) watermarked, two phosphor lines
(b) unwatermarked, two phosphor lines
*1s 3d green*
(a) watermarked, plain
(b) watermarked, two phosphor lines
*1s 6d greyish-blue*
(a) watermarked, two phosphor lines
(b) unwatermarked, two phosphor lines

Of these stamps, the 3d lilac with watermark and two phosphor lines is, in mint condition, the scarcest, though used specimens are common. Mint specimens are scarce because although on sale in Scotland for over two years, the stamps were not bought in large quantities by dealers and most were used on mail in the ordinary way. When collectors became more interested in stamps with phosphor lines, this variety was found to be in short supply.

Following the change to decimal currency on 15 February 1971 a new regional series was issued on 7 July 1971. These stamps had the profile portrait of the Queen by Arnold Machin, R.A., and the Rampant Lion of Scotland designed by Jefferey Matthews. Values were:

$2\frac{1}{2}$p pink
3p blue
5p pale violet
$7\frac{1}{2}$p light brown

All were on unwatermarked paper and had two phosphor lines, except the 2½p stamp, which had one.

To these distinctive Scottish stamps can be added a number of interesting and attractive pictorial issues with a close Scottish connection. These resulted from a radical change in stamp-issuing policy introduced by Mr. Anthony Wedgwood Benn, Postmaster-General in Mr. Harold Wilson's first Labour government. The criteria for deciding what subjects should be chosen for special issues of stamps had hitherto been very restricted. They were: (a) Royal anniversaries and occasions, (b) postal anniversaries and occasions, and (c) events of outstanding national or international importance. These criteria prevented the issue of stamps to honour famous men and women who were not members of the Royal Family or to celebrate the anniversaries of events which were not connected with either the Royal Family or the postal services. In December 1964 Mr. Wedgwood Benn announced the widening of the criteria so that stamps could be issued (a) to celebrate events of national and international importance, (b) to commemorate important anniversaries, (c) to reflect the British contribution to world affairs, including the arts and science, and (d) to extend public patronage to the arts by encouraging the development of minuscule art. The new criteria regularised a position which had become absurd. In April 1964, for example, stamps had been issued in all parts of the world to honour William Shakespeare on the 400th anniversary of his birth. Although a series of pictorials portraying Shakespeare and showing scenes from five of his plays had been issued in Britain, the Post Office had taken care to emphasise that these stamps were not intended to honour Shakespeare himself but to mark the international festival held at Stratford-upon-Avon in his memory. Mr. Wedgwood Benn followed this widening of the criteria, which removed such anomalies, by announcing in March 1965 that the Queen had consented to allow non-traditional as well as traditional designs to be submitted for her approval. This gave much greater scope to designers, the only stipulation being that the monarch's portrait, though no longer the dominant feature, must continue to be included in the design of all commemorative or pictorial stamps, as well as to be the main feature of the small definitive and regional stamps.

The reluctance of the Post Office to abandon its conservative stamp design and issue policy explains, though many Scots would consider it does not excuse, the long neglect of Scotland in the stamp album. Until 1966, indeed, no Scotsman had ever been portrayed on any stamp sold at his country's post offices. This was not for want of trying. In October 1955 Mr. Hector Hughes, Labour M.P. for North Aberdeen, asked whether the Postmaster-General, Dr. Charles Hill, would consider the issue in 1959 of a special stamp to celebrate the bicentenary of the birth of Robert Burns. Later the same year Sir Thomas Moore, Conservative M.P. for North Ayrshire, asked the same question and received the same answer: 'No!' In March 1958 Mr. Emrys Hughes, Labour M.P. for South Ayrshire, asked whether a specially designed greetings telegram might be issued for the bicentenary celebrations and the following month a deputation of both Houses of Parliament called on the Prime Minister, Mr. Harold Macmillan, and the Postmaster-General, Mr. Ernest Marples, to ask that the government's decision not to issue a Burns bicentenary stamp should be re-considered. Ten weeks later the Prime Minister gave his reply: 'No!' The bicentenary fell on a Sunday and as a special concession the post office at Alloway, Ayr, opposite the cottage where Burns had been born on 25 January 1759, was allowed to open during the morning so that postcards and envelopes posted there could be post-marked by hand on the anniversary. Normally mail posted at Alloway on Sunday was postmarked by machine in the head post office at Ayr, so the concession had little meaning for any-one but a student of postmarking practice. Despite this, there was considerable interest among collectors and the Alloway postmaster reported that he and his staff had to deal with almost 30,000 envelopes and postcards.

With the widening of the criteria for stamp issues following Mr. Anthony Wedgwood Benn's announcement in December 1964, the way was opened for Robert Burns at last to be portrayed on his country's stamps. The issue was made on 25 January 1966, the 207th anniversary of the poet's birth, and consisted of two values, 4d and 1s 3d, both designed by Gordon F. Huntly. The 4d stamp, coloured black, indigo and blue, had a portrait based on the Skirving chalk drawing and the 1s 3d stamp, in black, blue and orange, featured the Alexander Nasmyth portrait against a background symbolising Burns's life, a plough, a quill pen, a rose, a stook of barley, a thistle and the gable end of Mossgiel farmhouse.

In building a collection of British stamps with a Scottish association, it is probably better to group them according to their subjects rather than to arrange them in chronological order of their issue. Every collector has his own preferences but one convenient arrangement, allowing for expansion as more Scottish issues appear, falls into three categories: Famous Scots, Bonnie Scotland and The Scottish Story.

In the first category, with the stamps honouring Robert Burns, may be placed those portraying Queen Elizabeth, the Queen Mother. Born on 4 August 1900, she was the daughter of the Earl of Strathmore and Kinghorne. As Lady Elizabeth Bowes-Lyon she married the Duke of York on 26 April 1923 and when he succeeded to the throne as King George VI in December 1936, she became Queen Elizabeth. Their Coronation on 12 May 1937 was marked by the issue the following day of a special brown 1½d stamp showing their portraits. Queen Elizabeth was also portrayed on two stamps, 2½d blue and £1 dark blue, issued on 26 April 1948 in celebration of their Silver Wedding anniversary.

The next stamp devoted to a Scottish celebrity was a black and brown 7½p stamp issued on 28 July 1971 and portraying Sir Walter Scott as part of the celebrations of the bicentenary of his birth in Edinburgh on 15 August 1771. Although not portrayed in its design, Sir Alexander Fleming, the discoverer of penicillin, was honoured by a green and purple 1s stamp issued on 19 September 1967 in a series illustrating British discoveries and inventions. The design showed a penicillin mould, recalling the countless lives which have been saved by the work of the Scottish bacteriologist. He was born on 6 August 1881 at Lochfield, Darvel, in Ayrshire, and was educated at Kilmarnock Academy. A small portait of a Scottish-born airman, Arthur Whitten Brown, appeared on a multi-coloured 5d stamp issued on 2 April 1969 to mark the fiftieth anniversary of the first non-stop trans-Atlantic flight. Brown, born in 1886 in Glasgow, was navigator to John Alcock, who was portrayed on the stamp. Both were knighted and shared the *Daily Mail* prize of £10,000 for their pioneer flight in a converted Vimy bomber from Newfoundland to an Irish bog near Clifden, Co. Galway, in June 1919.

Stamps showing the sights and scenes of Bonnie Scotland provide the second category in a Scottish collection. All the issues belong to the reign of Queen Elizabeth II, beginning with the fine view of Edinburgh Castle which formed the design of the 10s stamp issued on 1 September 1955. This was one of four high value stamps all featuring British castles and the series remained in use until replaced in 1969 by the large stamps showing the profile portrait of the Queen by Arnold Machin. Collectors can identify three types of each of the castles stamps, one with a watermark consisting of an overall pattern of the royal cypher E 2 R with small crowns, the second with a watermark consisting of small crowns only, and the third without a watermark. The stamps were produced by three printers, Waterlow and Sons Ltd., Thomas De La Rue and Co. Ltd., and Bradbury,

Wilkinson Ltd., and specialist collectors can distinguish among their products by slight differences of paper, perforation and colour, as well as by minute variations in the engraving. *The British Commonwealth Stamp Catalogue* published by Stanley Gibbons Ltd. contains useful hints on the identification of the different printings.

The opening of the Forth Road Bridge was marked by the issue on 4 September 1964 of two special stamps, a 3d in black, blue and violet, and a 6d in black, blue and red. Designed by Andrew Restall, a former pupil of George Watson's College, Edinburgh, and later a student at Edinburgh College of Art, the stamps were modern in conception. The 3d stamp showed the Bridge with a tanker making its way to Grangemouth and a full moon above the snow-capped Lothian hills. The view on the 6d stamp was drawn from the south bank of the river and included the old railway bridge – *the* Forth Bridge to an older generation – in the background. Another bridge, that built in 1733 by General Wade across the Tay at Aberfeldy, was depicted on a multi-coloured 9d stamp issued on 29 April 1965. Also designed by Andrew Restall, the stamp was one of a series of four featuring British bridges.

An autumn view in the Cairngorms formed the design of a 1s 6d stamp in black, orange and blue, issued on 2 May 1966 as part of a series devoted to British landscapes. A line of bare black trees stands in the foreground, with snow-covered mountains rising in the distance. Another typically Scottish sight, a cottage with Fife harling, was depicted on a multi-coloured 5d stamp issued on 11 February 1970 in a series showing British domestic architecture. On a grander scale was the view of St. Giles's Cathedral, Edinburgh, on a 5d stamp issued in a series featuring British cathedrals on 28 May 1969. Below the profile portrait of the Queen at the right of the design was a tiny sketch of a stone angel which forms a roof boss in the Thistle chapel. In striking contrast was the view of the nuclear reactor at Doun-

reay, Caithness, seen on the multi-coloured 1s 6d stamp in a
series of four issued on 1 July 1964 to mark the twentieth International
Geographical Congress held in London during that
month. Stooks of corn in the foreground of the design emphasised
the difference between the traditional occupation of the
north-east and the new technology represented by the reactor.

The history of Scotland is not yet well proclaimed in the
stamp album. A multi-coloured 5d stamp was issued on 1 April
1970 to mark the 650th anniversary of the Declaration of
Arbroath. The design showed the scene in Arbroath Abbey as
King Robert the Bruce, large quill pen in hand, signed the letter
to Pope John XXII asserting Scotland's determination not to
submit to English domination. A much later period of Scottish
history was recalled by two of the six large stamps issued on 15
January 1969 in honour of famous British ships. One of the 9d
stamps showed the *Cutty Sark,* the record-breaking tea-clipper
launched at Dumbarton on 22 November 1869 and the 5d stamp
showed *R.M.S. Queen Elizabeth 2,* the Cunard Company's
65,800-ton liner launched on Clydebank by the Queen on 20
September 1967.

Although not directly related to Scotland, three series of
stamps issued to mark events for which Scotland was the host
country may also be included in a Scottish collection. Three
stamps, 2½d, 4d and 1s 6d, featuring lifeboatmen were issued
on 31 May 1963 to mark the ninth International Lifeboat Conference
held in Edinburgh. Four colourful stamps showing wild
flowers were issued on 5 August 1964 to mark the tenth International
Botanical Congress held in Edinburgh, values being
3d, 6d, 9d and 1s 3d. The ninth British Commonwealth Games,
also held in Edinburgh, were commemorated by three stamps,
5d, 1s 6d and 1s 9d, showing athletes in action, date of issue
being 15 July 1970.

This brief survey indicates that despite a dearth of Scottish
issues, careful selection and arrangement of the existing

material can produce an interesting and attractive display on a Scottish theme. With each year's programme of new issues, additions can be made to the collection and visual appeal can be improved by including some of the decorative souvenir envelopes or 'first day covers' which are marketed by the Post Office and by many private firms of philatelic publishers when new stamps are issued. Bearing the new stamps postmarked on the day they are placed on sale, these first day covers also have a vignette, a view or traditional emblems associated with the theme of the stamps themselves.

## The Postmark on a Letter

Ever since the earliest days of the postal service there have been complaints at delays in the delivery of mail. The first English Master of the Posts, Sir Brian Tuke, writing to Thomas Cromwell, Secretary of State to King Henry VIII, in August 1533, detailed the steps he was taking to ensure that the posts riding to Scotland should deliver their mail as promptly as possible. 'Surely', he wrote, 'the Posts northward, in time past, have been the most diligent of all other. Wherefore, supposing by my conjecture that the default is there, I incontinently sent through them a writing, sharp enough, showing their defaults, the King's high displeasure, and the danger.' For many years it was customary to augment the address of an urgent letter with such exhortations as 'Haste, post, haste! Haste for life, for life haste!' accompanied by vivid little sketches of a gallows with the corpse of some dilatory post-boy dangling from it. To such complaints we owe that familiar feature of the modern postal service, the postmark.

When Colonel Henry Bishop contracted to pay £21,500 per annum for the right to run the Post Office he cannot have envisaged the difficulties which were to beset him. One complaint was that before the mail from London reached Edinburgh the mail-bags were being opened by postmasters along the road, their usual excuse being that this was done by mistake because the bags were not properly labelled. To prevent this 'breaking open the Scotch Baggs' Bishop ordered every bag to be sealed with a brass tag bearing the name of the post town for which it was intended. He also required each postmaster to certify on the label that the seal was unbroken when the bag passed through his hands.

In reply to the perennial complaints of delays in the delivery of mail, Bishop announced that 'a stamp is invented that is putt upon every letter shewing the day of the moneth that every letter comes to the office, so that no Letter Carryer may dare detayne a letter from post to post, which before was usual'. Known to philatelists as the Bishop-mark, this stamp was a small circular or oval postmark divided across the centre by a horizontal line. In the upper half was the abbreviation for the month, JA for January, FE for February, and so on. In the lower half was a numeral representing the day. The Bishop-marks were introduced in London in 1661 and although Colonel Bishop relinquished his office as Postmaster-General two years later, the use of his marks continued, with modifications in their size and shape, until the early nineteenth century. The first Bishop-marks used in Edinburgh were slightly smaller than the London type and were oval instead of circular. Specimens on letters dated between 1693 and about 1720 are very scarce.

As the network of posts spread throughout the United Kingdom, postmarks became more informative. Those introduced by William Dockwra for his London Penny Post and by Peter Williamson for his Edinburgh Penny Post indicated whether postage had been prepaid or not and included the initial or name of the receiving-office where the letter had been posted. With the development of other local penny posts, postmarks were needed in many more towns and villages. Most of the early types simply showed the town's name in a straight line of capital letters but later types were circular or horse-shoe shaped. One of the latter used at Fort William had a decorative thistle in the centre but most designs were strictly utilitarian.

After the introduction of mail-coaches in 1784, postmarks with a figure representing the number of miles between the town and London were introduced to help postmasters to calculate the postage charge, then dependent on the distance a letter had to travel. Dumfries appears to have been the first town in Scotland to use one of these mileage marks, the number 341 being added in a box below the town's name. Later types were circular with the mileage figure in the centre and an initial letter signifying the principal post-town on the road along which the letter travelled. Among these route letters were B (Berwick), C (Carlisle), D (Dumfries), E (Edinburgh) and G (Glasgow). Another interesting postmark resulted from an Act of Parliament passed in 1813. Until then mail-coaches and other vehicles carrying the mail had been exempt from paying the tolls charged at toll-gates, turnpikes and bars. The turnpike trusts, which contracted for the upkeep of the roads in return for the income from the tolls, protested vehemently at the resulting loss to their revenues. Because of these protests the Act of 1813 ended the exemption on Scottish roads but so that the mails should not be delayed while the tolls were collected, the Edinburgh postmaster made an annual payment to the turnpike trusts. The Post Office was empowered to recover this amount by charging an extra halfpenny postage on every letter carried by a four-wheeled mail-coach on a Scottish toll-road. To show that the extra halfpenny was to be paid, letters were marked either with a '$\frac{1}{2}$' in manuscript or with a postmark reading 'Addl. $\frac{1}{2}$' or simply '$\frac{1}{2}$'. Most of the post-towns in Scotland were provided with one of these postmarks, as were a dozen English and Irish towns handling large quantities of Scottish mail. The use of the postmarks ended when the additional halfpenny postage was removed on 5 December 1839, with the introduction of a uniform postage rate of fourpence as a preliminary to Rowland Hill's uniform penny postage.

The issue in May 1840 of the Penny Blacks and Twopence

Blues brought a need for a new type of postmark, one which would prevent the stamps from being re-used by dishonest people. The design chosen is known to philatelists as a Maltese Cross, though it bears little resemblance to the emblem of the Knights of St. John of Jerusalem. The postmarkers were intended to be uniform but because they were hand made, usually of brass with a wooden handle, some differed noticeably from others. Experienced philatelists can identify the Maltese Cross postmarks of Stonehaven, in which the inner lines are thinner than normal, of Kilmarnock, which has a diamond-shaped dot in the centre, and of Greenock, Kelso, Montrose, Perth and Stirling by other slight variations in the design. These, with distinctive English and Irish types, are illustrated in the *Great Britain Specialised Stamp Catalogue, Volume I: Queen Victoria* published by Stanley Gibbons Ltd. Other varieties, some of them rare, are provided by the colour of the ink used for the Maltese Cross postmarks. The first to be used was red ink, which postmasters were instructed to make by mixing printers' red ink with linseed oil and sweet oil, but a more indelible black ink was later substituted so that the postmark could not be washed off the stamp. Some postmasters, through either carelessness or indifference, occasionally used ink of other colours. Examples of the Maltese Crosses struck in deep red at Aberdeen, in violet or magenta at Glasgow, in brown or slate-blue at Haddington and in orange-brown at Kircaldy are worth appreciably more than the normal red or black crosses used in most towns.

The Maltese Cross postmark had the disadvantage of giving no plain indication of the office where it was used. At the suggestion of Francis Abbott, later Secretary to the Post Office in Scotland, a new type of postmark was introduced in 1844. This incorporated a serial number which was allocated to each important office. Known to collectors, none too affectionately, as 'the Killer' because it effectively destroyed any beauty the stamp

might have possessed, the postmark consisted in Scotland of a
rectangle of thick horizontal bars with the office serial number
in the centre. In England and Wales the bars were arranged to
form an oval and in Ireland a diamond. As well as the postmark
cancelling the stamp on the front of the envelope, a circular
postmark giving the date and place of posting was usually struck
on the back, so that each letter had to be postmarked at least
twice. To obviate this extra work a new type of postmark was
introduced in 1853. This, known as the Duplex, combined the
Killer with the date-stamp bearing the office name. There were
many varieties of the Duplex postmarks. Some, used at Dundee,
Edinburgh and Greenock, had the date and name inside a
dotted circle. Between 1863 and 1873 another Duplex used at
Edinburgh consisted of the date-stamp combined with an ornamental cluster of bars, known as the Brunswick Star, with the
post office serial number 131 in the centre. This postmark was
first given its unusual name in the *Stamp Collector's Magazine*
for June 1863 and there has since been controversy over its
origin. The obvious explanation for the name seems to be the
most likely, that it derived from the Star of the Order of Henry
the Lion, an award for civil or military merit founded in 1834
by Duke William of Brunswick. The Brunswick family was well
known in Britain, Duke Karl having been killed in action
against the French at Quatre Bras, during the Waterloo campaign, and his daughter, Caroline of Brunswick, having been
the long-suffering wife of King George IV. A postmark used in
Glasgow had the date and name in a rectangle below the Killer
portion but in most types the date-stamp was in a circle with
the Killer at the right-hand side.

Another type of postmark particularly popular with collectors
was used at Scottish sub post offices between 1854 and 1860,
although examples dating back to 1841 are known. Mail collected at sub offices then, as today, was normally postmarked at
the district head office. But if a letter was being delivered locally

and did not pass through the head office, the stamp on it had to be postmarked in the sub office. For this purpose a postmark consisting simply of the office name was used. Most names were in a straight line of large capital letters but in a few cases the name was in a circle, among them Arrochar Village, Ardrishaig, Cumbernauld and Cambuslang. Because the amount of local mail was limited, neat and legible examples of these Scots Local Cancellations are scarce, especially on envelopes showing the complete name. A Broughty Ferry philatelist, Cecil W. Meredith, formed a fine collection which realised over £7,700 when sold at auction in April 1971. The highest price, £125, was paid for an envelope bearing a Penny Red stamp posted on 17 October 1841 at Strathmiglio, Fife, and with a Maltese Cross struck over the straight-line local postmark.

All these postmarks were struck by hand, so that collectors use the term 'hand-stamp' in referring to them, but during the 1870s the Post Office began experimenting with mechanical devices and machines which would apply the postmark automatically. The 1844 serial numbers continued to be used, especially in the machine postmarks cancelling bulk printed matter. A complete list of the numbers is to be found in *British Post Office Numbers, 1844-1906*, by G. Brumell, published by R. C. Alcock Ltd. The book gives details of the many changes and additions which have been made since the first list was published in 1844. The following is an abridged list which includes the postmarks most likely to be seen by collectors.

1 Aberdeen
2 Aberfeldy
3 Aberdour, Fife   later Achnacroish
4 Aboyne
5 Aberchirder   later Abernethy and Nethy Bridge
6 Alford
7 Alloa
8 Aberlour

5

9 Alexandria from 1887

10 Alness

11 Annan

13 Arbroath

15 Ardrossan

17 Airdrie

20 Arrochar   later Avoch

22 Anstruther

27 Ayr

31 Ballater

32 Crathie   later Bannockburn

33 Ballantrae

35 Banchory

36 Banff

37 Macduff   later Birnam

40 Beith

41 Biggar

44 Blair Atholl

46 Blairgowrie

56 Braemar   later Bothwell

57 Brechin

60 Bridge of Earn

61 Buckie

62 Burntisland

64 Callander

65 Campbeltown

67 Carluke

70 Carstairs from 1887

71 Castle Douglas

74 Coldstream

76 Carnoustie

80 Crail

82 Craigellachie

84 Crieff

86 Craigellachie Station from 1887
87 Cullen
88 Culross   later Corstorphine
90 Cumnock
92 Cupar
96 Cruden   later Cowdenbeath
98 Dalkeith
100 Dalmally
102 Denny
103 Dingwall
104 Dornoch
107 Doune
108 Dumfries
110 Dumbarton
111 Dunbar
112 Dunblane
113 Dunfermline
114 Dundee
115 Broughty Ferry
118 Dunkeld
119 Dunphail from 1887
121 Dunoon
123 Dunvegan
127 Dysart
130 Ecclefechan
131 Edinburgh
133 Elgin
134 Ellon
135 Elie
136 Errol
137 Evanton
138 Eyemouth
139 Falkirk
141 Fenwick

142 Fettercairn
143 Fochabers
144 Forfar
145 Forres
146 Fort Augustus
147 Fortrose
148 Fort William
149 Fort George
150 Fraserburgh
154 Fyvie
155 Galashiels
156 Garlieston   later Garmouth
158 Girvan
159 Glasgow
161 Grangemouth
163 Greenock
165 Glamis   later Garlieston
166 Grantown-on-Spey
167 Golspie
168 Brora
169 Gartly from 1887
171 Haddington
173 Hamilton
174 Hawick
175 Helmsdale
176 Helensburgh
177 Harris   later Holytown
178 Huntly
179 Holytown   later Innellan
181 Inverary
182 Inverkeithing
183 Inverness
185 Invergordon
186 Irvine

187 Johnstone   later Innerwick
190 Jura
192 Keith
193 Kelso
198 Killin
200 Kingussie
201 Kintore
202 Kilsyth   later Kirn
203 Kilmarnock
204 Kincardine   later Kilwinning
205 Kinghorn
206 Kinross
207 Kirkwall
209 Kirkcudbright
210 Kirkcaldy
211 Kirkintulloch   name changed to Kirkintilloch, 1887
212 Kirriemuir
215 Lanark
216 Langholm
217 Largs   later Upper Largs
221 Leith
227 Lochearnhead
229 Leven
230 Linlithgow
237 Lairg
240 Lybster
241 Markinch
244 Melrose
248 Mintlaw
249 Methlick   later Macduff
251 Montrose
256 Moffat
263 Musselburgh
264 Nairn

265 Newburgh
267 New Deer   later Newington
268 New Pitsligo   later Newmilns
270 Newton Stewart
273 Oban
274 Old Meldrum
275 Old Rain   later Old Aberdeen
277 Paisley
279 Peebles
280 Perth
281 Peterhead
282 Pitcaple
283 Pittenweem
284 Pitlochry
285 Poolewe
287 Port Glasgow
288 Port Patrick   later Port of Monteith Station
289 Portree
290 Portsoy
295 Renfrew
296 Rhynie
297 Rothes
298 Rothesay
299 Rothiemay   later Rogart
300 St. Andrews
302 Saltcoats
303 Sanquhar
305 Selkirk
306 South Queensferry
308 Stirling
309 Stonehaven
310 Stornoway
312 Stranraer
313 Strathaven

314 Strathdon
316 Stromness
320 Tain
321 Tarbert   later Muir of Ord
324 Thurso
325 Tobermory
326 Tomintoul   later Tayport
328 Tongue   later Taynuilt
330 Troon
331 Turriff
334 Ullapool
336 West Kilbride   later Windygates
337 Whitburn   later West Kilbride
339 Wick
341 Wigtown
342 Wishaw

The 1844 list ended with Wishaw. Later changes and additions included:

346 North Berwick from 1845
347 Penicuik from 1845
348 Portobello from 1845
349 Prestonpans from 1845
358 Tillicoultry from 1856
361 Motherwell from 1856
364 Bridge of Allan from 1857
366 Insch from 1857
369 Coatbridge from 1874
375 Partick from 1874
379 Aviemore from 1874
385 Leslie from 1874
389 Alva from 1874
390 Dollar from 1874
392 Muthill from 1874
397 Govan from 1874

400 Shotts from 1874
406 Johnstone from 1874
409 Larbert from 1874
448 Strathpeffer from 1887
459 Kincardine from 1887
481 Roxburgh from 1887
504 Dalmeny from 1887
532 Lhanbryde from 1887
540 Archiestown from 1892
575 Aberfoyle from 1892
589 Aberdour from 1892
601 Rum from 1892
639 Tomintoul from 1892
686 Maud from 1906
695 Glenfinnan from 1906
705 Kincardine from 1906
710 New Lanark from 1906
726 Aberchirder from 1906
727 Cambuslang from 1906
733 Rosehearty from 1906
741 Roseneath from 1906
755 Canna from 1906

## A Lady's Love Letters

Many a stamp collection owes its gems to the prudence of lawyers and the imprudence of lovers. The deed-boxes of Victorian offices and the writing desks of Victorian sitting rooms have yielded treasures galore to delight the eye of the philatelist, simply because lawyers and lovers made a practice of preserving their correspondence. Few can have paid as heavy a penalty for doing so as did a young Frenchman who died in agony in his Glasgow bedroom on 23 March 1857.

Pierre Emile L'Angelier was the son of a French nurseryman who had settled in Jersey after the Paris revolution against King Charles X in 1830. Pierre was apprenticed to the same trade, first in Jersey and later with a firm of seedsmen in Edinburgh. He spent some time in France during the 1848 revolution against King Louis Philippe but returned to Scotland and eventually found employment as a packing-clerk with a Glasgow firm of seed merchants. Early in 1855 he made the acquaintance of Madeleine Smith, one of the daughters of a well-to-do city architect named James Smith.

Madeleine was a vivacious and attractive girl of nineteen living with her parents, brothers and sisters in India Street, Glasgow. The family kept several servants so that Madeleine had little to occupy her time except the conventional round of social activities and long holidays at the Smith's villa, Rowaleyn, at Rhu, on the Gareloch. L'Angelier was older than Madeleine, he was considered charming and handsome, and he had a background, particularly in his experiences in a Paris twice torn by revolution, which must have set him apart from most of Madeleine's young men friends. Although as a clerk earning no more than a pound a week, with no capital and few prospects, he was unlikely to be considered by her parents as an acceptable suitor, Madeleine fell in love with him. At first they were able to meet only occasionally while walking in the street but Madeleine spent much of her spare time writing long and affectionate letters, to which L'Angelier replied in equally amorous terms.

In the spring of 1855 Mr. Smith learned that Madeleine and her sister Bessie had been seen walking with a young man who was not known to him. In deference to his forcibly expressed wishes Madeleine made a half-hearted attempt to end her association with L'Angelier but the decision was short-lived and by enlisting the aid of one of the Smith's housemaids and of an elderly spinster friend of L'Angelier she and her suitor were able to continue exchanging letters. A few weeks later L'Angelier asked Madeleine to marry him but her father's consent was out of the question and in September she wrote to L'Angelier breaking off their correspondence and asking him to burn all her letters to him. At the same time she wrote explaining her reasons to the spinster friend, Miss Mary Perry. 'Emile will tell you that I have bid him adieu. My Papa would not give his consent so I am in duty bound to obey him. Comfort dear Emile. It is a heavy blow to us both . . . Think not my conduct unkind,' she concluded. 'I have a father to please, and a kind father, too.'

Madeleine destroyed the letters she received from L'Angelier but he made drafts of some which he considered important and from one of these it appears that his reply to her letter of adieu contained a threat. 'You have deceived your father as you have deceived me,' he wrote. 'You never told how solemnly you bound yourself to me, or if you had, for the honour of his daughter he could not have asked you to break off an engagement such as ours. Madeleine, you have truly acted wrong . . . but I give you my word of honour I shall act always as a gentleman towards you.' Then came the threat. 'Think what your father would say if I sent him your letters for perusal. Do you think he could sanction your breaking your promises? No, Madeleine, I leave your conscience to speak for itself.'

Whether or not Madeleine was influenced by this threat there is no way of telling but she resumed her regular correspondence with L'Angelier in even more affectionate terms and by the end of the year she was addressing him as 'my own darling husband' and signing herself 'thy own dear loving wife' or 'thy own Mimi L'Angelier'. There was talk of elopement, of publishing banns of marriage and of the possibility of a clandestine wedding in Edinburgh. None of these plans came to fruition but when Madeleine went to Rowaleyn for the spring and summer of 1856, L'Angelier visited her there and they found ample opportunity at last to become lovers. Madeleine's letters and a draft of one to her from L'Angelier suggest that he felt more remorse than she did at this climax in their relationship but although they both spoke of trying to control their desires, their resolution wavered and their intimacy continued.

In November 1856 the Smiths moved to 7 Blythswood Square, Glasgow, a corner house in which Madeleine occupied a basement bedroom. Next door lived a wealthy city merchant named William Minnoch, fifteen years older than Madeleine and an eligible bachelor. Although L'Angelier left letters, unobtrusively sealed in brown envelopes, on the window sill of Madeline's bedroom and was occasionally admitted to the house under cover of darkness for hasty love-making or to drink a cup of coffee or chocolate, her passion for him began to wane. Moreover William Minnoch began to pay court to her and on 28 January 1857, with the approval of her parents, Madeleine accepted his proposal of marriage. A few days later she made another attempt to end her liaison with L'Angelier. She used as an excuse the fact that he had returned one of her letters, probably in a fit of pique because it was less ardent than those he had been accustomed to receive. 'When you are not pleased with the letters I send you, then our correspondence shall be at an end,' she wrote icily, 'and as there is coolness on both sides, our engagement had better be broken.' She added a peremptory request for the return of all her previous letters. Apparently receiving no reply to this request, she wrote again a few days later, a curt note asking him either to bring the letters himself or to send them by post in a parcel addressed to the housemaid who was in Madeleine's confidence.

There is no trace of L'Angelier's reply to these two requests but that it frightened Madeleine almost out of her wits is obvious from the hysterical letter she wrote on 10 February. She pleaded with him not to send her letters to her father, reiterating that although her love for him had cooled there was no question of her loving anyone else. Another letter, longer but in similar tone, followed. 'I could stand anything but my father's hot displeasure, Emile, you will not cause me death,' she wrote. 'If he is to get your letters, I cannot see him any more. And my poor mother – I will never more kiss her. It would be a shame to them all.' Then the hysteria seems to have subsided and Madeleine wrote in more balanced terms, less passionate but full of endearments, asking only for the return of the letters she had written recently. On Thursday, 19 February, her desperate dilemma still unresolved, Madeleine went with William Minnoch and his sister to the theatre. An Italian opera company had presented *La Traviata* on the first three nights of that week but it was not until Sir Compton Mackenzie, about twenty-five years ago, searched among old play-bills in the Mitchell Library, Glasgow, that the name of the opera performed on that Thursday evening was recalled. It was Gaetano Donizetti's *Lucrezia Borgia.*

Next morning L'Angelier's landlady found him ill in bed, having been violently sick during the night. He spoke of suffering severe stomach pains the previous night while on his way home but he did not mention where he had been. The following day, 21 February, Madeleine visited a chemist's, Murdoch Brothers in Sauchiehall Street, and bought an ounce of arsenic. She told the chemist that it was needed for killing rats at Rowaleyn though she later changed her story to claim that she wanted the arsenic as a cosmetic. In his diary for 22 February L'Angelier noted: 'Saw Mimi in the drawing room. Promised me French Bible. Taken very ill.' His landlady found him in his bedroom, early in the morning of 23 February, writhing in agony with stomach pains and a bilious attack which for a week prevented him from going to work.

At the beginning of March, Madeleine was to spend a few days at Bridge of Allan. She wrote to L'Angelier, urging him also to take a short holiday, preferably in the south of England. 'Stirling you need not go to,' she wrote, 'as it is a nasty dirty little town.' The day before her departure she bought another ounce of arsenic at the shop of John Currie and Son in Sauchiehall Street, again ostensibly for killing rats. Her holiday was enlivened by a visit from William Minnoch during the course of which they agreed to arrange their wedding for a day in June. After Minnoch had returned to Glasgow, Madeleine wrote a prim but affectionate letter to him, expressing her 'warmest, kindest love' and adding 'Our walk to Dunblane I shall ever remember with pleasure. That walk fixed a day on which we are to begin a new life, a life which I hope may be of happiness and long duration to both of us.'

Madeleine does not appear to have met L'Angelier either at Bridge of Allan or on her return to Glasgow but on 18 March she bought a third ounce of arsenic at Currie's shop. Three days later she wrote her last letter to L'Angelier, an impassioned note urging him to see her. 'Why my beloved did you not come to me. Oh beloved are you ill? Come to me sweet one,' she pleaded. 'I waited and waited for you but you came not. I shall wait again tomorrow night, same hour and arrangement. Do come sweet love my own dear love of a sweetheart . . . Adieu, with tender embraces, ever believe me to be your own ever dear fond Mimi.' This letter was postmarked on 21 March and L'Angelier left his lodgings the following evening at about nine o'clock. Five hours later, early in the morning of Sunday, 22 March, his landlady was awakened by the ringing of her door-bell. She found L'Angelier in agony on the door-step and despite the attentions of two doctors he died the next day.

A post-mortem, asked for by L'Angelier's employers, revealed that death was due to arsenical poisoning, about 88 grains, at least twenty times the fatal dose, being found in the dead man's stomach. Among his possessions at his lodgings were the letters Madeleine had written to him, almost two hundred over a period of two years. As soon as enquiries began, first by a member of the French consulate and then by the Procurator-fiscal, Madeleine fled to Rowaleyn but William Minnoch and one of her brothers followed her and brought her home to Glasgow. On 7 April she was arrested and charged on three counts, of administering arsenic with intent to poison L'Angelier on 19 or 20 February 1857, of again administering arsenic with intent to poison him on 22 or 23 February, and of murdering him by the same means on 22 or 23 March 1857.

The trial began on 30 June at the Court of Sessions in Edinburgh. There were some strange features. The diary kept by L'Angelier, in which he recorded his meetings with Madeleine, was not admitted as evidence, a serious handicap, since the Crown case depended upon being able to prove that Madeleine and L'Angelier had met immediately before each alleged attempt to poison him. Madeleine's behaviour was remarkably composed and confident for a person on trial for her life. The *Ayrshire Express* described her as having 'the air of a belle entering a ballroom' and the *Glasgow Mail* reported that 'the utmost coolness is stated to have been manifested by the prisoner ever since she was placed in custody'.

On the first charge the Crown was unable to provide evidence that L'Angelier had met Madeleine on the night of her visit to the opera, 19 February. He had mentioned to Miss Perry two days earlier that he hoped to meet Madeleine on that evening but the latter denied that the meeting had taken place. Another difficulty was that the Crown could find no evidence that Madeleine had possessed any arsenic or other poison at that time. The Lord Justice-Clerk therefore directed the jury to find the accused Not Guilty on the first charge. The Dean of Faculty succinctly expressed the Crown's dilemma. 'Either L'Angelier was ill from arsenical poisoning on the morning of the 20th or he was not,' said the Dean. 'If he was, he had received arsenic from other hands than the prisoner's. If he was not, the whole foundation of the case is shaken.' The dilemma might have seemed less real had the diary kept by L'Angelier been admitted as evidence. One entry read: 'Thurs. 19 Feb. Saw Mimi a few moments, was very ill during the night.'

The second charge depended for proof on the postmark of a letter written by Madeleine to L'Angelier. The Crown sought to show that the lovers had met on the night of Sunday, 22 February, a few hours before L'Angelier's second and more serious attack of vomiting and internal pains. In the absence of the diary, in which L'Angelier had recorded the meeting and his illness, the only admissible evidence was a letter written by Madeleine in which she referred to the previous Sunday night's meeting. But the letter was headed only 'Wednesday' and bore no date, so that there was no indication of which Sunday she was mentioning. The postmark, of the Glasgow rectangular Duplex type, had been struck so carelessly that it was virtually illegible. The comptroller of the sorting office in the Glasgow Post Office, who rejoiced in the name of Rowland Hill Macdonald, was called to give evidence. Of the postmark in question he said: 'I found this one illegible. The figures must have been 2 or 20 something. It may have been the 2nd of February; if not the 2nd it is about the 20th.' He also believed that the abbreviation for the month included the letter R, which would have eliminated February as the month when the letter was posted.

In reply to questions from the Lord Justice-Clerk, Mr. Macdonald agreed that instructions had been given in the sorting office that letters should be postmarked more carefully. 'What you have seen in this case,' added the Lord Justice-Clerk, 'will suggest the desirableness of this; and you had better give my compliments to Mr. Abbott and tell him he had better give further instructions to the Scots offices.' Mr. Francis Abbott was the Secretary to the Post Office in Scotland and had previously advocated the introduction of the 1844 post office serial numbers. In his address to the jury the Dean of Faculty referred at length to the illegible postmark. 'The only date the letter bears is "Wednesday",' he said, 'and it may be, so far as the letter is traced, any Wednesday in the whole course of their correspondence. There is not a bit of internal evidence in this letter, nor in the place where it was found, to fix its date, unless you take that reference to Friday night, which is, of course, begging the whole question. Therefore, I say again, gentlemen, that it might have been written on any Wednesday during the whole course of their correspondence and connection. But it is found in an envelope from which its date is surmised. And, gentlemen, you are to be asked to convict, and to convict of murder, on that evidence alone. I say that if this letter had been found in an envelope bearing the most legible possible postmark, it would have been absurd and monstrous to convict on such evidence, but when the postmark is absolutely illegible, how much is that difficulty and absurdity increased? Except that the Crown witness from the Post Office says the mark of the month has an R, and that the post office mark for February has

*James Burnie Esq*

*Kirkcudbright*

W. MULREADY. R.A.

POSTAGE ONE PENNY.

JOHN THOMPSON.

20th INTERNATIONAL GEOGRAPHICAL CONGRESS **1 6**

PENICILLIN **1/-** HARRISON

The Cairngorms SCOTLAND L ROSOMAN HARRISON AND SONS LTD **1.s 6d**

Fife harling **5d**

**5ᵈ** ST. GILES' EDINBURGH

Robert Burns HUNTLY HARRISON AND SONS LTD **1/3**

Sir Walter Scott 1771/1832 **7 1/2 p**

Aberfeldy Bridge 1733 RESTALL **9d**

NINTH INTERNATIONAL LIFE-BOAT CONFERENCE **4d**

FORTH ROAD BRIDGE 1964 **3d**

POSTAGE REVENUE **3d**

POSTAGE **10/-**

**5ᴾ**

POSTAGE REVENUE **9d**

E·R POSTAGE REVENUE

*Above* Designs suggested by C. P. Rang for British pictorial stamps: the Highlands and Edinburgh.

*Centre* James Chalmers' suggested penny stamp, 1838; Edinburgh 'Brunswick Star' postmark, 1870; Edinburgh 'Duplex' postmark, 1890.

*Below* 'N. Buchanan' signed this photograph of a Post Office staff about 1910 but omitted to note its whereabouts!

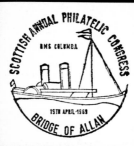

*1st row*   Aberdeen, Idaho; Inverness, 1905; Banff, Alberta.
*2nd row*   Scottish Philatelic Congress, Bridge of Allan, 1969, *R.M.S. Columba*; Additional
½d, 1813-1839; Post Office Philatelic Bureau frank, Edinburgh, 1972.
*3rd row*   Dundee, Mississippi; Elgin, Illinois.
*4th row*   Scottish Philatelic Congress, Bridge of Allan, 1965; Aboyne Games centenary, 1967.

BALLATER 17 AUGUST

1967 HIGHLAND GAMES

Miss Alys Shearer,
I, Linn Crescent,
BUCKIE.
Banffshire.

SCOTTISH PHILATELIC CONGRESS 1971

UNIVERSITY OF STIRLING

BEARSDEN AND STIRLING

PHILATELIC SOCIETIES

C. W. Hill
Philatelic Correspondent
THE OBSERVER
160 Queen Victoria Street

London E.C.4

*Above* Ballater Highland Games, 1967.
*Below* Scottish Philatelic Congress, University of Stirling, 1971.

THE·POST
FOR·ALL·KENT
GOES·EVERY
NIGHT·FROM
THE·ROVND·HO·
VSE·IN·LOVE·
LANE & COMES
EVERY·MOR
(NING)

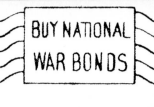

BUY NATIONAL
WAR BONDS

Prestwick
FOR GOLF

PRESTWICK
2 -PM
26 JLY
1965
AYRSHIRE

Live to Learn
Learn to Live
EDINBURGH ROAD
SAFETY CAMPAIGN

EDINBURGH
5 30PM
19 OCT
1964
B

**ELGIN**
bids you
welcome

**BUCKHAVEN**
& **METHIL**
FOR
**INDUSTRIAL EXPANSION**

DUNDEE

A CENTRE OF INDUSTRY

DUNDEE, ANGUS
1150M
1 JNE
1964
A

*Stranraer*
in Bonnie Galloway

RACING
AT AYR
THE IDEAL HOLIDAY

Glasgow Exhibition.    14/9/02    Love from Greta    Main Building.

Scotch Express leaving Carlisle Station

The Wrench Series No. 4510

*Above*    Glasgow Exhibition, 1901, main building.
*Below*    'Scotch Express leaving Carlisle Station' 1904 (Wrench series).

*Above*  The Clyde Shipping Company's *S.S. Dungeness,* 1905. 'Coasting Tours, England, Scotland, Ireland'.
*Below*  The Carron Line's *S.S. Avon*, *c.* 1910. 'London and Scotland—best and quickest route to Glasgow via Firth of Forth—steamers passing under Forth Bridge.'

'Post from Crieff'—concertina views, 1918, with a postwoman of the First World War

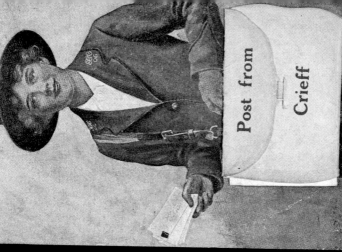

'Scottish Life and Character'—Highland telegraph girl, 1912 (Raphael Tuck and Sons

HIGHLAND TELEGRAPH GIRL

*1st row*    Andrew Carnegie (U.S.A.), William C. Cowie (North Borneo), *S.S. Lady McLeod* (Trinidad), Lord Byron (Greece).

*2nd row*    R. L. Stevenson (Western Samoa), Lord Cochrane (Chile), Mungo Park (The Gambia).

*3rd row*    Robert Burns (U.S.S.R.), Robert Burns (Romania), *Peter Pan* (New Zealand), Lord Byron (Italy).

*4th row*    King James VI (Barbuda), Lord Byron (Greece), Alexander Graham Bell (Canada).

# CINDERELLA STAMPS

*1st row*    Tanera More, plaice; Stroma, Churchill; Carruthers Bus Service.
*2nd row*    Scottish National Party, William Wallace and St. Andrew; Pabay, crab.
*3rd row*    Glasgow Area 1971 Strike Post; Scottish Secretariat, Robert Burns; St. Kilda 'specimen', shag.
*4th row*    Sanda, puffin; David MacBrayne Ltd; W. Alexander and Sons (Northern) Ltd.

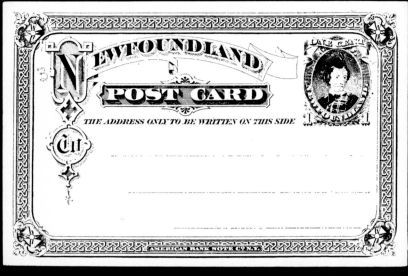

*Above* Colonel Bishop and the Edinburgh Bishop-mark, 1693, on a publicity label of 1960; David Livingstone on a 10s. booklet cover.

*Centre* Regional designs on a Scotex souvenir sheet, 1962.

*Below* The Prince of Wales (later King Edward VII) in Highland dress on a Newfoundland 1-cent postcard, 1880.

no R, we have no evidence even as to the month. My learned friend must condemn the evidence of his own witness before he can fix the postmark.' In short, concluded the Dean of Faculty, 'the envelope proves absolutely nothing'.

In his charge to the jury the Lord Justice-Clerk spoke scathingly of the postmarks. 'I trust', he said, 'that this will be the last occasion on which the postmarks are so carelessly impressed as they have been. You see the large number of marks which are so illegible that the dates cannot be ascertained; in some cases the year being illegible, in others the month, and in others the day of the month. All this is done in Glasgow in a most careless and slovenly manner. It is a very important matter for the ends of civil and criminal justice that the postmarks should be properly stamped. Mr. Macdonald says that strict instructions have been given on this point, and that new stamps have been furnished in many instances; and I hope the attention of the Post Office authorities will be still more directed to a matter of such great importance.' On the second charge the jury returned a verdict of Not Proven. The court had not seen two other entries for 1857 in L'Angelier's inadmissible diary: '*Tues. 24 Feb.* Wrote M. *Wed. 25 Feb.* M wrote me.'

The Crown case on the third charge failed on similar grounds. There was clear evidence of a motive for Madeleine to murder her lover, since he held letters so compromising to her, but there was no irrefutable evidence that the two lovers had met on the night of 22 March. For at least five hours of that evening, indeed, L'Angelier's movements could not be traced. In *Not Proven*, published in 1960 by Secker and Warburg, the author, John Gray Wilson, cogently summarises the evidence of the many witnesses called by prosecution and defence in an attempt to prove or disprove a meeting on that night. The gaps and discrepancies in this evidence were the reason for the verdict returned by the jury on the third charge. It was Not Proven, by a majority.

Madeleine Smith's trial was the sensation of mid-Victorian Scotland and argument over her guilt or innocence has raged perennially ever since. She herself was married twice, though not to William Minnoch, and she eventually settled in the United States, where she died in April 1928 at the age of ninety-two. The Glasgow rectangular Duplex postmarks whose illegibility had been so important a factor in her defence were withdrawn from use within a few weeks of her acquittal. But because of their dramatic associations the postmarks remain firm favourites with philatelists, to whom they are always known, quite simply, as 'the Madeleine Smiths'.

## Postmarks tell the World

Postmarks enjoining the public to 'Post early for Christmas' or 'Express good wishes by greetings telegram' or 'Remember to use the Post Code' are so familiar a feature of the modern postal service that it is difficult to realise they originated over three hundred years ago. As well as introducing the first date-stamps, known to philatelists as the Bishop-marks, the indefatigable Cavalier Colonel Henry Bishop also introduced the first slogan postmarks. Since he was paying £21,500 per year for the right to run the Post Office, it was in Colonel Bishop's interest that the postal services should be used as widely as possible in preference to the privately organised rival services which caused a serious loss of revenue to the Post Office. The slogan postmark was one of Colonel Bishop's weapons. The first advertised the daily posts on the Dover Road. It was circular, measuring about 1¼ inches in diameter, and the slogan was in nine horizontal lines of capitals, 'The post for all Kent goes every night from the Round House in Love Lane and comes every morning'. Letters bearing this slogan are rare and a clearly struck example on a letter which also bore the small Bishop-mark of 24 August 1661 was sold by Robson Lowe Ltd. at an auction in 1962 for £450.

After Colonel Bishop had relinquished his appointment as Postmaster-General, two more circular slogans were introduced. Both advertising the posts along the Norwich and Colchester Road, they read 'Essex Post goes and coms every day' and 'S.X.

Post comes every day 1675'. Examples of the former have been found on letters dated 1674 and there are several examples of the latter among the State Papers in the Public Record Office, London, but both are very scarce.

Despite the obvious advantages of advertising the postal services by eye-catching and informative slogans, almost two and a half centuries elapsed before the scheme was revived. In November 1917 *The Times* carried a small news item describing and illustrating a slogan postmark being used in the United States to advertise war savings. 'Buy Now – U.S. Government Bonds—2nd Liberty Loan', it read. Prompted by this, the British Post Office introduced a similar postmark. The slogan, reading 'Buy National War Bonds Now', was first used in London on 10 December 1917 and similar postmarks, 'Feed the Guns with War Bonds' and 'Buy National War Bonds', were used the following year at head post offices in all parts of the United Kingdom.

After the war slogans continued to be used on a modest scale to publicise the British Industries Fair and the British Empire Exhibition held at Wembley in 1924 and 1925, as well as to persuade the public to 'Post early in the day', to 'Cable to Canada, Australia and New Zealand via Imperial' or to 'Join the King's Roll and employ War Disabled Men'. The telephone service was widely advertised between 1926 and 1936 by such slogans as 'Say it by telephone', 'Every home needs a telephone', 'Shop by telephone' and 'The telephone makes life easier', all of which were used at Scottish as well as at other British post offices. A distinctive Scottish slogan was that used during 1938 to advertise the 'Empire Exhibition Glasgow, May - October 1938'. This may be claimed as the earliest Scottish pictorial slogan, for it had an angular but spirited rampant lion in its design.

The outbreak of the Second World War brought a fresh crop of slogans at Scottish and other offices to exhort Britons to

'Grow more Food—Dig for Victory', to 'Help to win on the Kitchen Front' and to 'Save Waste Paper Metals Bones Rags'. The end of the war was celebrated by slogans reading 'Victory in Europe', 'Victory over Japan' and by one without words but with a large V above two gaily ringing bells and wavy lines consisting of the three dots and a dash which represent V in the Morse Code. The post-war austerity years were chronicled by such slogans as 'Don't waste bread – others need it', 'Lend a Hand on the Land', 'Save your waste paper for salvage' and 'Save for the Silver Lining'. Pealing bells again appeared in a pictorial slogan which showed the initials E and P in a lovers' knot to celebrate the wedding of Princess Elizabeth and Prince Philip in 1947 and there were some wry smiles when the income tax demand notes sent out by Scottish inland revenue offices that year were occasionally seen to be postmarked with a slogan reading 'Blood donors are still urgently needed'.

In 1948 the first slogans advertising the Edinburgh Festival were used at about twenty of the larger Scottish post offices. They read 'International Festival – Music and Drama – Edinburgh 22nd Aug to 12th Sept' and similar slogans were used again, with slight modifications, in 1949 and 1950. The Scottish Industries Exhibition held in Glasgow in 1949 was also publicised by a postmark reading 'Scottish Industries Exhibition – Glasgow – 1st to 17th Sept 1949'.

Until 1956 slogan postmarks were used only for government-sponsored campaigns for which nation-wide publicity was required but in that year the General Post Office decided to allow postmarks to commemorate events or to mark anniversaries of a local character. Hand-stamped postmarks had already been used on many occasions for this purpose but the first local machine-stamped publicity slogan was used in September 1956 to celebrate the centenary of the incorporation of the borough of Rochdale, Lancs. This was followed in 1957 by several similar postmarks, including one to celebrate the centenary of the burgh of Johnstone, Renfrewshire. Neat, clear impressions of this Johnstone postmark are not easy to find as it was in use only from 24 to 31 December. A local slogan with a different purpose was 'Let's stamp out T.B. – X-Ray Glasgow, March 11 – April 12', used at post offices in the Glasgow area during that period in 1957. A similar slogan, 'X-Ray Motherwell & Wishaw, Sept 15 to Oct 3' was used in 1958. There was a pictorial slogan in 1959 to mark the 150th anniversary of the National Bible Society. Showing an open Bible with the globe and St. Andrew's Cross behind it, the slogan read 'National Bible Society of Scotland, 1809-1959'.

A further relaxation of the regulations governing the use of slogan postmarks was announced in 1963, when local authorities were permitted to sponsor postmarks advertising the tourist attractions or commercial and industrial amenities of their towns. The first pictorial postmark for tourist publicity was introduced at Hastings, Sussex, on 1 April 1963 and featured a cheerful Saxon warrior polishing his helmet beside the sea, with the slogan 'We're ready for your invasion at Hastings'. This was followed later in the year by the first Scottish tourist slogans. These, with the periods in 1963 and 1964 when they were first used, were:

> 'Come to Stirling' 24 June to 29 September 1963 and 1 December 1963 to 29 February 1964
> 'Edinburgh, capital by the sea for festival and holiday 19 August 1963 to 18 October 1964
> 'Tourist camping Wick' 19 August 1963 to 18 August 1964
> 'Holiday at Dunoon' 1 October 1963 to 30 September 1965
> 'Ski-centre Pitlochry' 1 November 1963 to 29 February 1964 and 1 to 30 November 1964
> 'Inverness the Highland Capital' 1 December 1963 to 1 December 1965
> 'Dunbar for happy Holidays' 8 December 1963 to 7 December 1965

'Girvan's Atlantic breezes stop winter sneezes' 9 March
to 5 July 1964

'Elgin bids you welcome' 2 March 1964 to 1 March 1965

'Holiday in Pitlochry' March, May, July, September 1964

'Pitlochry your Tourist Centre' April, June, August,
October 1964

'Pitlochry Centre for Ski-ing' 1 December 1964 to 28 February 1965

'Prestwick Indoor Bowls' 26 October 1964 to 16 January
1965

Kelso used two wordless publicity postmarks, one showing a
fishing scene and the town's distinctive Maltese Cross postmark
of 1840 (9 March 1964 to 30 April 1964) and the other with a
picture of Kelso Abbey and bridge (1 May to 2 August 1964 and
2 November 1964 to 3 January 1965).

Meanwhile slogan postmarks were being introduced to publicise other aspects of Scottish towns. The first were:

'Midlothian for Industrial Sites' 2 December 1963 to 31
May 1964

'Buckhaven & Methil for industrial expansion' 12 February 1964 to 11 February 1966

'Greenock's dry dock for the Giants' 1 April to 31 July
1964

'For new industry, Glasgow, industrial enquiries centre'
6 April to 5 October 1964

'Expand in Alloa' 20 April 1964 to 19 April 1965

'Dundee – a centre of industry' 1 June 1964 to 31 May
1965

'Greenock, the town whose products span the world' 1
August to 31 December 1964

These lists of the first machine-stamped publicity postmarks
used in the campaign to attract tourists and industries to Scotland may be completed by adding those which commemorated

specifically Scottish anniversaries or events during 1963 and
1964. They included:

'G.J.C.C. Road Safety Week, March 16-23, Let Glasgow
Flourish – Safely' March 1963

'1163 Paisley Abbey 1963 – 800th Anniversary' 9 September to 20 October and 2 December to 29 December 1963

'Learn to Swim Week – Scotland 25th-30th May 1964' used
at Aberdeen, Ayr, Dumfries, Edinburgh N.W.D.O.,
Falkirk, Glasgow, Motherwell, Perth and Paisley 25
to 30 May 1964

'Kirkintilloch 750th Anniversary 1214-1964' 30 April to
31 December 1964

'Scottish Epilepsy Week 15-22 March 1964 – Epilepsy
Everybody's Business' Edinburgh and Glasgow, 8 to
22 March 1964

'Live to Learn – Learn to Live – Edinburgh Road Safety
Campaign' Edinburgh, 19 October to 1 November
1964

'Your Life's in your hands – Edinburgh Road Safety Campaign' 2 to 15 November 1964

'Live! and Let Live' – Edinburgh Road Safety Campaign'
16 to 29 November 1964

Some slogan postmarks have, inevitably, aroused controversy,
despite the care taken by the Post Office to avoid giving offence.
World Refugee Year, staged during 1959 and 1960 by the
United Nations Organisation, was publicised in Britain by a
postmark which included a drawing of an outstretched hand
with fingers extended. Unfortunately when the postmark was
struck so that the hand fell near to the Royal portrait on a
stamp, the Queen seemed to be making a most unregal gesture.
After comment in newspapers and protests from the public the
slogan was re-designed to omit the offending hand. In 1965 the
Post Office had to segregate mail despatched by a London firm
of philatelic auctioneers when one of its directors pointed out

that the letters were being postmarked by a slogan advertising an exhibition organised by a rival firm to mark the centenary of its stamp catalogues. Arrangements for centralising the handling of mail in Morayshire led in August 1971 to strong complaints in Forres, one of the towns affected by the new scheme. Letters from the town were being taken to Elgin for postmarking and sorting but instead of receiving a postmark advertising the holiday attractions of Forres, the letters were being postmarked 'Elgin bids you welcome'. Complaints from Forres councillors led to the withdrawal of the unwelcome slogan.

The overall size of these slogan postmarks was about 3½ inches long by 1 inch wide and they consisted of two parts, the circular date-stamp at the left giving the name of the post office and the date, and at the right the slogan itself. In 1961 the Philatelic Congress of Great Britain, the organisation which links British philatelic societies and meets annually to discuss matters affecting the hobby, suggested to the Postmaster General that the arrangement of the slogan postmarks was unsatisfactory. Pointing out that a part of the slogan was normally illegible because it fell on the stamp, the Congress urged that the positions of the date-stamp and the slogan should be reversed so that the latter fell clear of the stamp. After some consideration the Post Office agreed to do this and the new arrangement, known to philatelists as 'transposed', has been used for many slogan postmarks since 1962. As an inexpensive means of publicity the slogans have proved increasingly popular and so many different types are now being used that assembling a complete collection would be a formidable undertaking. Most collectors content themselves with a representative selection, perhaps of slogans supporting a particular campaign or publicising certain events, or of those used in a favourite Scottish town or county. The usual practice is to cut the slogan from its envelope in a rectangle of about 4 inches by 1½ inches or 2 inches, taking care to include the date-stamp portion and the postage stamp. Because they are much scarcer, it is considered preferable to preserve slogans dating from before about 1930 on the complete envelopes.

Philatelists make an arbitrary distinction between machine-printed slogan postmarks and postmarks stamped by hand. Colonel Bishop's slogans of 1661 were hand-stamped but their age and scarcity would qualify them for inclusion even in a collection otherwise devoted to machine-made postmarks. Equally diverse and interesting are the hand-stamps which have been used to postmark mail posted at such events as exhibitions, trade fairs, agricultural shows, congresses and conferences. The first publicity or commemorative postmark of this kind is generally agreed to have been used at the International Exhibition held from May to November 1862 in South Kensington. The first Scottish exhibition postmark was used in July 1888 at the Glasgow Exhibition and this was followed by a similar postmark used at the Edinburgh International Exhibition in 1890. Among other events for which hand-stamped postmarks were used during the period before the First World War, when a major exhibition was staged somewhere in Britain almost every year, were the following:

Glasgow Exhibition   May to October 1901

International Engineering Congress, Glasgow   September 1901

Scottish National Exhibition, Edinburgh   May to October 1908

Church of Scotland General Assembly, Edinburgh   May 1910

Scottish National Exhibition, Glasgow   May to October 1911

Royal Highland Show, Inverness   July 1911

Fifth Philatelic Congress of Great Britain, Edinburgh   23 to 25 August 1913

Since the Second World War many of these commemorative hand-stamps have been pictorial in design, often featuring

Scottish motifs or coats-of-arms. Those used at the Ballater Highland Games, for example, have depicted a thistle (1964), deer (1965), blackcock in flight (1966), a piper (1967) and similar Highland devices. Others have remained strictly utilitarian, consisting simply of the normal circular date-stamp. As well as the distinctive postmarks used on mail carried by sea, rail or air, which are mentioned in other chapters, there are many categories of Scottish postmark which offer possibilities for study. Interesting collections can be formed of postmarks connected with the following events or used by the types of post office listed:

The Royal Highland Show, recorded as having a circular date-stamp with the words 'Showyard – Inverness in July 1911 and having its first pictorial hand-stamp, showing the Highland Society's coat-of-arms and the words 'Royal Highland Show, Ingliston, Newbridge, Midlothian', in June 1962

The General Assembly of the Church of Scotland, recorded as having a circular date-stamp with the words 'Edinburgh C S' in May 1910 and similar postmarks in subsequent years

Highland Games, such as those at Aberdeen and Ballater

Philatelic congresses and exhibitions

Hotel post offices, such as Gleneagles, Perthshire, the Ardwell Inn, Stranraer, and the Hydropathic, Crieff.

Post offices attached to railway stations

The post offices of the Islands

Post offices associated with Scottish celebrities, such as Bannockburn (Robert the Bruce), Alloway (Robert Burns) and Lossiemouth (Ramsay MacDonald)

Post offices with the names of battles, such as Killiecrankie, Prestonpans and Culloden Moor

Extra illustration material is provided, in the case of many modern hand-stamps, by the decorative envelopes published in connection with the event or anniversary which the postmarks commemorate. These envelopes usually have an appropriate design or picture printed on the front, at the left-hand side, leaving space at the right-hand side for the addressee's name and address, the postage stamp and the special postmark. Some towns have publicised their attractions and amenities by envelopes bearing views and a few words of advertisement. During the 1950s, for example, Buckie was tempting holiday-makers by envelopes with a map of northern Scotland showing the town's position, small black-and-white views of the main shopping centre, the harbour or the Strathlene beach, and above them the invitation to visit 'Buckie on the Moray Firth for Holidays'. Such envelopes, usually discarded as of little philatelic interest when first introduced, eventually become accepted as collectors' items, especially if they have a clear postmark of the town they are advertising.

Postmarks dating from the period before such souvenir and publicity envelopes were used may be accompanied instead by a selection of old picture postcard views or of the souvenir postcards publicising exhibitions and other events. An interesting collection can be formed by combining picture postcards showing views of post offices with specimens of the postmarks which have been used at the same offices. Views dating from Queen Victoria's reign, which ended in January 1901, are scarce but views of Edwardian post offices are more plentiful because the heyday of the picture postcard coincided with the reign of King Edward VII, from 1901 to 1910. The views of the larger post offices in busy towns are remarkable for the absence of motor vehicles, early twentieth-century transport being represented as a general rule by a tram or two, a few horse-drays and hansom-cabs, and the ubiquitous boy on a bicycle. In views of the smaller post offices the staff usually had time to stand at the door while the photographer focussed his camera, and sometimes a wee message-boy with a few minutes to spare in those more leisurely days gives an unauthorised grin from the side of the picture. The Post Office policy of concentrating mail at head offices for postmarking and sorting has resulted in the small local offices ceasing to postmark much of the mail passing through them, so that neat and legible postmarks of small post offices are becoming much more elusive than they were.

In 1966 the *Post Office Magazine* appealed for claimants to the title of 'the oldest post office in Britain', by which was meant the building where Post Office business had been transacted without a break for the longest period of time. One claimant with a long history was the Edinburgh General Post Office, whose foundation stone was laid by Albert, the Prince Consort, on 23 October 1861, shortly before his death, and which was opened in May 1866. Exactly a century later Prince Philip opened the modernised public counter and office. The Edderton sub post office, in Ross-shire, and several English post offices were able to claim continuous service since the 1840s but far out-distancing all of them was the sub post office at Sandquhar, Dumfries. The earliest reference to this was an entry in the *Edinburgh Almanack* of 1763, which announced that the post for Sandquhar left Edinburgh at nine o'clock on Saturday evenings, arriving back in Edinburgh on the following Friday afternoon. By 1788 Sandquhar was receiving a post from Edinburgh three times a week. The title deeds of the post office premises date from 1760 and the name of John Halliday, who is known to have been the postmaster of Sandquhar, appears on the deeds in 1809. There was little doubt that the Sandquhar post office had occupied the same premises without a break since about 1800 and probably for at least forty years before that date. It was, by a long way, 'the oldest post office in Britain'.

As well as postcard views of post offices such as Sandquhar, with a place in postal history, those of towns or villages with unusual names provide an amusing theme for a collection. Christian names are well represented in Scottish postmarks.

There is a Leslie in Fife and another near Insch, in Aberdeenshire; Gordon is to be found on the Borders where the Gordons originated, in Berwickshire; Keith is in Banffshire and Kirk further north, in Caithness, while every Aberdonian knows where to find Kittybrewster. There is a story behind each of the place-names which recall the clans and lairds whose homes they once were, among them Campbeltown, Gordonstoun, Fraserburgh, Dufftown and Grantown-on-Spey.

But there is no need for the collector of postmarks with a Scottish association to confine his search to those used only in Scotland. Wherever Scots have settled, in the United States, in Canada, in South Africa, in Australia or New Zealand, from Minto, Alaska, in the north to the South Shetlands in Antarctica, they have left their mark on the map and their postmark in the stamp album. There are Aberdeens in Idaho, Kentucky, Maryland, Mississippi, North Carolina, Ohio, South Dakota and Washington, as well as in Nova Scotia, New South Wales, South Australia, Cape Province, Jamaica and Sierra Leone. Dundee is to be found in nine American states and Elgin in the same number, though Glasgow appears to have given its name to only six American towns with their own post offices. There are postmarks which show Dunfermline in Illinois, Cullen in Louisiana, Montrose in Arkansas and Culloden in West Virginia, while ten states have a Glencoe of their own. The official list of post offices in the state of North Dakota includes some names which would certainly repay further research, so many of them are of Scottish origin. They include Abercrombie, Ayr, Bathgate, Buchanan, Caledonia, Clyde, Elgin, Hamilton, Kelso, Kintyre, McGregor, McKenzie, McLeod, Perth and Ross. It is obvious that North Dakota's rolling fields of oats, barley and wheat, even its pit-heads in the western highlands, must have reminded many exiled Scots of the fields and hills of home.

## Letters on the Railway

Railways and postage stamps evolved together, vehicles for that expansion of commerce and industry which made Victorian Britain the wonder of the civilised world. The mail-coach was still in its heyday when the first bags of mail were carried on the Liverpool and Manchester Railway soon after its opening in September 1830. Coach and train combined to speed the mail from London to Liverpool even before the railway between London and Birmingham had been completed. On 3 July 1837 a mail-coach left the General Post Office in St. Martin's-le-Grand at eight o'clock in the evening and arrived early the following morning in Birmingham. From there the mail was carried by the Grand Junction Railway to Liverpool, arriving at half-past twelve in the afternoon. The whole journey had taken sixteen and a half hours, a saving of five hours over the mail-coach service.

The success of this experimental run led to the suggestion that one of the railway carriages should be fitted out as a sorting office so that mail could be sorted and prepared for delivery during the journey. The first carriage, a converted horse-box, made its trial run between Birmingham and Liverpool on 6 January 1838 and proved so successful that specially designed sorting carriages were built and brought into service within a few months. They were fitted with counters, desks and pigeon-holes, and lit by oil lamps. An apparatus devised by a post office inspector, John Ramsey, enabled bags of mail to be taken on board while the train was in motion. Bags of mail ready for delivery en route were simply thrown out of the carriage window.

On 17 September 1838 the London and Birmingham line was completed. The railway post offices, or travelling post offices as they were later called, were then able to run from London to Liverpool, serving Manchester, Warrington and other northern industrial towns linked by the rapidly expanding railways. During the 1840's the 'railway mania' led to the amalgamation of many small companies and the extension of main lines into Scotland. The Caledonian Railway Company was formed in 1845 and opened its line from Carlisle to Beattock in September 1847. It reached Glasgow five months later, the branch from Carstairs Junction to Edinburgh being opened at the same time, and the line was extended to Perth during the following year. In 1846 Parliament authorised the creation of the Great Northern Railway's line from King's Cross to York and in 1848 the York, Newcastle and Berwick Railway Company was formed to control 360 miles of line which had been built by eight smaller companies. Thus steadily the network spread across the countryside, drawing local lines into the main systems. In June 1862, while Abraham Lincoln was still the President of the United States and there was still a Bonaparte on the throne of France, an express train began leaving King's Cross every weekday morning at ten o'clock for Edinburgh's Waverley Station, 393 miles away. The *Flying Scotsman*, as the express came to be called, was the East Coast rival to the West Coast's Euston-to-Glasgow express, which had a longer but not unbroken history and did not receive its title of *Royal Scot* until after the First World War. One of the minor mysteries of philately is linked, literally as well as metaphorically, to the *Flying Scotsman*. The 5-centavos stamp in a series issued in Uruguay in 1895 showed a locomotive clearly identifiable as one of the Great Northern Railway's Stirling class 4-2-2 eight-footers, which hauled the *Flying Scotsman* during the 1880s and 1890s. These locomotives had never been used in Uruguay and the clue to the strange choice of design probably lies in the fact that the printers of the stamps, Waterlow and Sons Ltd., also printed the stationery of the Great Northern Railway.

As the main-line railways reached into Scotland, the railway post offices followed. The first was the Caledonian travelling post office which began to run between Carlisle and Glasgow on 10 March 1848, and others were soon operating between Perth and Carlisle, Ayr and Carlisle, Edinburgh and Carlisle, and Edinburgh and Glasgow. It is ironical that the first distinctive postmarks used by the sorters in the travelling post offices were to identify letters which had been mis-sorted and should not have reached the travelling post offices. Such postmarks read 'Missent to Railway Post Office' or 'Missent to G.N. Railway Post Office – Day', or have simply the initials of the railway company, 'C.R.' or 'North W-Ry'.

In 1859 the Post Office decided that mail handled in the travelling post offices should have distinctive postmarks in addition to those applied in the post office receiving the mail for the first sorting. At first these postmarks gave only the initials of the railway company but more informative postmarks were soon introduced. They were usually circular, showing the name of the travelling post office and the date. Typical examples read 'Edinr. M' in the 1860s, 'Caledonian T.P.O. – Night Up' and 'Edinr. – Carlisle Sorting Tender' in the 1870s. The Duplex type of postmark was also introduced during the 1870s, that of the 'Edinr. – Carlisle Sorting Tender' having the number of the Edinburgh head office, 131, in thin bars at the side, and the 'Highland S.T.' having the number 391 allocated to it. The term 'sorting tender', changed in 1904 to 'sorting carriage', referred to the fitted coaches which were considered as branches of the head office which controlled their operations and which provided the staff to man them. The railway post offices, or trav-

7

elling post offices, on the contrary, were controlled from London and had no special connection with any other head office. Philatelists now usually apply the term 'T.P.O.' equally to both.

As well as the sorting carriages and travelling post offices which were attached to normal passenger trains, the Post Office made use of Limited Mail trains. These were run primarily for the transport of mail but were also permitted, hence their name, to carry a limited number of passengers. The first of these trains set out from Euston on 1 February 1859 for Aberdeen. The acceleration in the delivery of mail by this service was detailed in the *Tenth Report of the Postmaster-General, on the Post Office,* presented to Parliament by Lord Stanley of Alderley in 1864. As the Postmaster-General explained, 'In 1854 a letter despatched from London to Edinburgh or Glasgow by the Night Mail of Monday would not have been delivered until about noon on Tuesday. There would then have been an interval of only two hours between the delivery of the letter and the despatch of the next Mail to London.' In normal circumstances the reply could not have been posted until Tuesday evening and would not have been delivered in London until Wednesday afternoon. As a result of the introduction of the Limited Mail service, however, there was time for a reply to be prepared in normal business hours to catch the Edinburgh or Glasgow Night Mail on Tuesday evening and to be delivered in London before business hours began on Wednesday morning.

'But', went on the Postmaster-General, 'the effect of the acceleration on the correspondence of places lying north, of Edinburgh is still more remarkable. In 1854, a letter despatched from London to Aberdeen by the Night Mail of Monday would not have arrived in Aberdeen until 5 p.m. on Tuesday. A reply might have been despatched from Aberdeen at 8.40 on Wednesday morning; but it will be obvious that the interval between 5 p.m. and 8 a.m. could not conveniently be employed for business purposes. If, however, the reply had been despatched from

Aberdeen on Wednesday morning, it would not have been delivered in London until Thursday morning. Now, if a letter be despatched from London to Aberdeen on Monday night, it is delivered in Aberdeen soon after noon on Tuesday, and the reply may be written during the hours of business, and despatched on Tuesday, so as to reach London in time for delivery before noon on Wednesday. Thus the time required for the transmission of a letter from London to Aberdeen, and for the receipt of a reply, has since the beginning of the year 1859 been shortened, for all practical purposes, to the extent of one day.' The postage on a letter sent by this service, it will be recalled, was still one penny.

On 1 July 1885 the Aberdeen Limited Mail was replaced by the Special Mail, a train which was not intended to carry passengers and was entirely devoted to the work of the Post Office. This was one of four which have played a vital part in the rapid distribution of mail in the United Kingdom. They are the Down Special, from Euston to Aberdeen; the Up Special, from Aberdeen to Euston; the Great Western Down, from Paddington, London, to Penzance; and the Great Western Up, from Penzance to Paddington. The two last-named replaced the London and Exeter travelling post office and the Cornwall sorting tender in 1895.

In his book *The Post Office*, published in 1927 by G. P. Putnam's Sons, Ltd., Sir Evelyn Murray, then Secretary to the Post Office, gave a graphic account of the work of the Up Special during its run from Aberdeen to Euston. It was the last train from the north able to connect with the early morning deliveries in the Midlands, the Home Counties and London. As well as mail sorted in the Aberdeen head office, bags from the Buchan and Elgin lines were taken on board before the train, with its staff of seven sorters, left Aberdeen at 3.25 p.m. En route to Stirling mails from thirty towns were received either by the automatic apparatus or at brief scheduled stops. At Law Junction a travelling post office from Glasgow, staffed by twenty-four men, joined the Up Special, bringing with it mail from Glasgow and the Western Highlands. At Carstairs the Edinburgh, Leith and Midlothian mails were taken on board. During these stages of the journey the mail destined for Perth, Stirling, Glasgow and Edinburgh was sorted and disembarked at the appropriate stations.

At Carlisle mails from about sixty towns in southern Scotland, Northumberland and Cumberland, and from the Ayr-to-Carlisle travelling post office, were taken on board, the staff now numbering fifty men in about a dozen coaches, later to be increased to sixteen. Of these coaches, five were each allocated to a particular division of the country and post offices sending mail to be picked up by the train sorted it according to these divisions. At Preston more north of England mail was received and at Warrington the mails for Northern Ireland were transferred to a train connecting with the Stranraer-to-Larne steamer, while those for the Irish Free State were despatched to Chester to join the Irish Mail on its way from Euston to Holyhead.

At nineteen minutes past midnight the Up Special steamed into Crewe, then regarded as 'the night mail capital of the United Kingdom'. Mail was transferred to thirteen travelling post offices based on Crewe and other mail was taken on board, having been brought by the travelling post offices from wide areas of Wales, the Welsh Marches, the Black Country, Birmingham and even from as far north as York. The next stop was at Tamworth to pick up the mails from the East Midlands and Lincolnshire, and to despatch mail for those areas, some of it by the Tamworth-to-Lincoln travelling post office. At Rugby the mails for East Anglia and the southern Midlands were despatched and the late night mail from Birmingham was received. Finally, between Rugby and Euston, the staff sorted mail for London and beyond, meanwhile dropping off bags at intermediate stations by means of the automatic apparatus. At 3.55

a.m., just twelve and a half hours after leaving Aberdeen, the Up Special would steam into Euston, bringing some 2,500 bags of mail for which Post Office vans were already waiting. Much of the London mail was delivered at breakfast-time while four travelling post offices, bound for Bristol, Bournemouth, Ipswich and Leeds, took on board other bags which the Up Special had brought south.

The number of travelling post offices and their time-tables have naturally changed considerably over the years. One which had a comparatively short life was the Fife Sorting Tender, which began running in December 1884 from Tayport to Burntisland, to handle mails between Edinburgh and Dundee before the opening of the second Tay Bridge in 1887 and of the Forth Bridge in 1890. It ceased running in November 1915.

During the 1930s there were over seventy travelling post offices in operation, including the following which served Scotland:

Ayr – Carlisle Railway Sorting Carriage

Caledonian Travelling Post Office Day Down (Carlisle to Perth)

Caledonian T.P.O. Day Up E (Edinburgh to Carstairs)

Caledonian T.P.O. Day Up GW (Glasgow to Carstairs)

Caledonian T.P.O. Day Up (Perth to Carlisle, including the two previous T.P.O.s which joined at Carstairs)

Carlisle – Ayr R.S.C.

Carlisle – Edinburgh Sorting Carriage (formed part of Down Special)

Crewe – Glasgow R.S.C. (formed part of Down Special between Crewe and Carstairs)

Down Special T.P.O. (Euston to Aberdeen and Glasgow, the two sections separating at Carstairs)

Edinburgh – York T.P.O.

Galloway T.P.O. Down Night (Carlisle to Stranraer)

Galloway T.P.O. Up Day (Stranraer to Carlisle)

Highland T.P.O. Down (Perth to Helmsdale)

Highland T.P.O. Up (Northern section, Helmsdale to Dingwall)

Highland T.P.O. Up (Southern section, Dingwall to Perth)

London – York – Edinburgh T.P.O.

North-Eastern T.P.O. Night Down (King's Cross to Newcastle-upon-Tyne and Edinburgh)

North-Eastern T.P.O. Night Up (Newcastle-upon-Tyne to
King's Cross)

North-Eastern T.P.O. Night Up Z (Leeds section, joining
Newcastle section at Doncaster to form one train to King's
Cross)

North-Western T.P.O. Night Down (Euston to Carlisle)

Up Special (Aberdeen to Euston, Joined at Law Junction
by Up Special G T.P.O. from Glasgow and at Carstairs
by Up Special E.H. from Edinburgh to form one train
to Euston)

On 21 September 1940 all the sorting carriages and travelling
post offices were suspended because of the war. The Down
Special and the Up Special continued to run but carrying only
sealed mail bags, no sorting being done on board. Both resumed
normal working on 1 October 1945 and other travelling post
offices were gradually restored, so that by October 1946 forty-
three of the seventy or so services operating before the war had
been re-introduced. The most notable absentees were the Galloway travelling post offices between Carlisle and Stranraer,
which had begun operating in 1871. A newcomer, on 10 September 1951, was the Manchester to Glasgow sorting carriage.
By 1955 fifty-one travelling post offices were in operation. One
whose time-table included some particularly evocative names
was the Highland T.P.O. Down. This had originated in 1864 as
the Highland Sorting Carriage running between Inverness and
Aviemore. It had been extended south to Perth in 1870 and
north to Helmsdale in 1873, being given its modern title of
Highland T.P.O. in 1930. It was due to leave Perth twenty-two

minutes after the arrival there of the Down Special, from which
it received some of its mail. It then ran as follows:

| | |
|---|---|
| 6.47 a.m. | Perth |
| 7.29 | Pitlochry |
| 7.41 | Blair Atholl |
| 8.27 | Dalwhinnie |
| 8.43 | Newtonmore |
| 8.49 | Kingussie |
| 9.07 | Aviemore |
| 9.25 | Carr Bridge |
| 10.12 | Inverness |
| 10.45 | Clunes |
| 10.50 | Beauly |
| 11.02 | Conon |
| 11.08 | Dingwall |
| 10.40 | Evanton |
| 11.47 | Alness |
| 11.54 | Invergordon |
| 12.05 p.m. | Kildary |
| 12.13 | Fearn |
| 12.21 | Tain |
| 12.36 | Edderton |
| 12.58 | Bonar Bridge |
| 1.06 | Culrain |
| 1.09 | Invershin |
| 1.24 | Lairg |
| 1.43 | Rogart |
| 1.51 | The Mound Junction |
| 1.59 | Golspie |
| 2.13 | Brora |
| 2.23 | Loth |
| 2.34 | Helmsdale |

For many years it has been possible to post mail in special posting boxes provided on travelling post offices or in the booking-

hall of the terminus stations. A small charge, the Late Fee, was payable on each letter in addition to the normal postage. On 1 March 1880 the Late Fee was fixed at a halfpenny prepaid, like the postage, by ordinary postage stamps. If a letter was posted in one of the special boxes without the Late Fee being added, it was surcharged double on delivery to the addressee. Registered mail and recorded delivery packets were also accepted before the departure of the travelling post office. An extra fee was required, the amount in 1970 being 1s 6d, prepaid in stamps which had to be affixed before the letter was presented at the travelling post office.

The philatelic interest of the travelling post offices lies mainly in the postmarks which have been used in them since the 1850s. Most of these have been the ordinary circular date-stamps, recognisable by the names of the terminus stations, by the initials S.C. (sorting carriage), S.T. (sorting tender), R.S.C. (railway sorting carriage) or T.P.O. (travelling post office), or by the title of the T.P.O. itself, such as 'Down Special', 'London – York – Edinburgh', or 'Highland T.P.O. Up – Southern Section'. Envelopes with such postmarks dating from before the First World War are scarce and some of the Victorian postmarks on complete envelopes are very rare. Even part of such a postmark on a stamp which has been removed from its envelope is often considered worthy of a place in a collection devoted to railway philately, simply because the collector may be unable to obtain a specimen on a complete envelope. Many collectors combine a selection of the postmarks with picture postcards or photographs of the locomotives which have powered the travelling post offices.

A closely related philatelic field of study is provided by the railway letter stamps issued by Scottish as well as other British railway companies. Although the companies ran goods and parcels services, they were not permitted to organise their own letter service, since the collection and delivery of letters was a

Post Office monopoly. But by tying a piece of string round a letter, this could be regarded as a parcel and the railway company could accept it for onward despatch by the next available train to the station nearest its destination. Here it could be collected by the addressee at a considerable saving of time over the normal post office delivery. In 1891 the Post Office acknowledged the impossibility of enforcing its monopoly of letter mail by agreeing to allow the railway companies to organise what was known as the Railway Letter Service. From 1 February 1891 any company authorised to act as the agent of the Postmaster General could accept and convey letters at a fee of twopence in addition to the normal postage of one penny. To prepay the fee, the railway companies were empowered to issue their own stamps. These were in a large square design, almost all of them printed in green, with the figure of value in the centre, the name of the railway concerned, and the inscription 'Fee for conveyance of single post letter by railway'.

Franked by a railway letter stamp and the ordinary postage stamp, the letter was accepted by the company, despatched to the station nearest its destination and there either collected by the addressee or posted for delivery by the post office in the usual way. On 15 January 1920 the railway letter fee was raised from 2d to 3d, and on 1 September 1920 to 4d. It was lowered to 3d on 1 January 1928 and again raised to 4d in 1940. These changes resulted in the issue of new stamps, still in the same basic design but with different face values, or in the surcharging of the older issues to adjust their face value to the correct rate. After the Railways Act of 1921 had grouped over 120 separate companies into four main systems, the London, Midland and Scottish Railway, the London and North Eastern Railway, the Great Western Railway and the Southern Railway, the railway letter stamps were gradually discontinued. By 1940, when very few railway letters were being despatched, ordinary railway parcels stamps were generally used on the letters also. The nationalisation of British Railways on 1 January 1948 spelled the final disappearance of the railway letter stamps from normal commercial use. They have since been revived, as a means of raising funds, by some of the small, privately-run English and Welsh narrow-gauge railways. British Railways still operate the railway letter service but ordinary postage stamps are used to prepay the whole fee. Early examples of the railway letter stamps used on complete envelopes are now scarce and some of the stamps of the smaller railway companies are rare because so few were issued. The following is a simplified list of the stamps issued by Scottish companies and by companies operating into Scotland:

Ayrshire and Wigtownshire Railway
> 2d green

Caledonian Railway
> 2d green
> 3d green
> 4d green

City of Glasgow Union Railway
> 2d green

Dumbarton and Balloch Joint Line
> 2d green
> 3d green
> 4d green

Dundee and Arbroath Joint Railway
> 2d green
> 2d red
> 3d red
> 4d red

Glasgow and South Western Railway
> 2d green
> 3d green
> 4d green

Glasgow, Barrhead and Kilmarnock Joint Railway
  2d green
  3d surcharged on 2d green
  3d green
  4d green
Great Northern Railway
  2d green
  2d red and black
  3d red and black
  4d red and black
Great North of Scotland Railway
  2d green
  3d green
  4d surcharged on 3d green
The Highland Railway
  2d green
  3d green
  3d greenish-yellow
  4d green
Invergarry and Fort Augustus Railway
  2d green
London, Midland and Scottish Railway
  4d green
London and North Eastern Railway
  4d greenish-yellow
  4d green
  4d blue
North British Railway
  2d green
  2d grey
  3d green
  4d greenish-yellow
  4d blue

Portpatrick and Girvan Joint Line
  2d green
Portpatrick and Wigtownshire Railway
(later Portpatrick and Wigtownshire Joint Railways)
  2d green
  3d blue
  4d blue

A collection of railway philately can also be augmented by some of the souvenir envelopes which are issued occasionally to mark special events. On 26 October 1968 Engine No. 4472, *Flying Scotsman*, made its last run on British Railways before being refitted and shipped to the United States to make a six months' tour to publicise an exports campaign. For the run, from Liverpool to Carlisle, a travelling post office was attached to the train. Souvenir envelopes with a picture of the *Flying Scotsman* were placed on sale to commemorate the run and the special postmark read 'Moorlands Rail Tour – Flying Scotsman – 26.10.68 – Carlisle'. The following year another souvenir envelope was issued to mark the locomotive's run from London to Liverpool en route for the United States. On this occasion a postmark reading 'Flying Scotsman – Departure 19 Sep 1969 – Liverpool' was used. Such envelopes make a colourful contrast to the more prosaic covers in which most letters make their journey. Suitably annotated with brief explanatory captions, they provide a display of interest to both philatelist and layman.

With the increasing use of road vehicles and aircraft for moving mail within the United Kingdom, the future of the travelling post offices is becoming more uncertain. The railway train, and particularly the Night Mail, awakens the same emotions, a mixture of pride, awe and nostalgia, as the mail-coach aroused in the hearts of Britons a century and a half ago. W. H. Auden has expertly caught this mood, as well as the rhythm of the train itself, in the poem he wrote as part of the

commentary to the film *Night Mail*, produced in 1936 by the
G.P.O. Film Unit under the direction of John Grierson.

'This is the night mail crossing the border,
Bringing the cheque and the postal order,
Letters for the rich, letters for the poor,
The shop at the corner and the girl next door.
Pulling up Beattock, a steady climb –
The gradient's against her but she's on time.

Past cotton grass and moorland boulder,
Shovelling white steam over her shoulder,
Snorting noisily as she passes
Silent miles of wind-bent grasses.
Birds turn their heads as she approaches,
Stare from the bushes at her blank faced coaches.
Sheepdogs cannot turn her course,
They slumber on with paws across.
In the farm she passes no one wakes,
But a jug in the bedroom gently shakes.

Dawns freshens, the climb is done.
Down towards Glasgow she descends
Towards the steam tugs yelping down the glade of cranes,
Towards the fields of apparatus, the furnaces
Set on the dark plain like gigantic chessmen.
All Scotland waits for her:
In the dark glens, beside the pale-green lochs,
Men long for news . . .

Letters from uncles, cousins and aunts,
Letters to Scotland from the South of France,
Letters of condolence to Highlands and Lowlands,
Notes from overseas to Hebrides
Written on paper of every hue,
The pink, the violet, the white and the blue,

The chatty, the catty, the boring, adoring,
The cold and official and the heart's outpouring,
Clever, stupid, short and long
The typed and the printed and the spelt all wrong.

Thousands are still asleep
Dreaming of terrifying monsters,
Or a friendly tea beside the band at Cranston's or
    Crawford's;
Asleep in working Glasgow, asleep in well-set Edinburgh,
Asleep in granite Aberdeen.
They continue their dreams;
But shall wake soon and long for letters,
And none will hear the postman's knock
Without a quickening of the heart,
For who can hear and feel himself forgotten?'

## Letters over the Water

If the early postal services within the United Kingdom were slow and expensive, those which linked Britain with countries overseas and with her own off-shore islands were even slower, more expensive and more hazardous. The Dover Road, by which mail travelled between London and the continent, was the most important route and during the reign of King Henry VIII one of the cross-Channel vessels was appropriately named the *Post Horse*. There was another continental mail route between Harwich and the Netherlands, while Falmouth was chosen as the main port for the West Indies, North America and the Mediterranean. Most of the ships used for these services were yachts or hoys of between 20 and 50 tons, with a crew of six or eight and capable of carrying a dozen or two passengers. They were known as packet-boats or packets.

The conquest of Ireland during the reign of Queen Elizabeth I and the conflict between Cromwell and the Irish supporters of King Charles I made regular postal services to Ireland a military necessity as well as a commercial convenience. Holyhead was the main port for Dublin, Milford Haven for Waterford, and Portpatrick was chosen as one terminus for the short sea route across the North Channel to Donaghadee. The Scottish Parliament's Post Office Act of 1695 ordered that packet-boats should provide a regular service on this route. Queen Anne's Act of 1711, combining the English and Scottish Post Offices, confirmed the service and settled the postage for the crossing at 2d, payable in addition to the normal inland postage. One result was the improvement of the posts between Portpatrick and Edinburgh, Ayr and Glasgow. In 1825 paddle-steamers replaced the sailing-packets but as steamers increased in size the mail and passenger services were transferred to Stranraer, where there were better harbour facilities. Few letters despatched by the Portpatrick to Donaghadee packets bear any postmark signifying their route, mainly because the mail-bags were not opened until they reached Belfast or Dublin in Ireland and Glasgow or Edinburgh in Scotland. A straight-line postmark with the word 'Ireland' in capitals and another with the name 'Port Patrick' in two lines of capitals were used, the former briefly in the late eighteenth century and the latter for nearly forty years at the beginning of the nineteenth century. More usually the clues are provided by the address from which the letter is written, its destination, any endorsements on the outside and the post office clerk's scribbled calculation of the amount of postage due.

Without the stimulus of military or commercial necessity, postal services for the Scottish islands lagged far behind those for other overseas destinations and there were few satisfactory services until towards the end of the eighteenth century. One of the earliest was organised soon after the Forty-Five to link Lewis with the mainland. From Stornoway a sailing-packet landed the mail at Poolewe, from where it was taken by the foot-post to Inverness. The Post Office made a contribution towards the cost of the packet and of the foot-post, while the Earl of Seaforth, the proprietor of Lewis, paid most of the balance. But it was not until 1834 that a regular weekly service to Lewis was finally established. By this time, mail brought by the foot-post from Poolewe to Achnasheen could there be handed over to the horse-post running on the new road from Loch Carron via Achnasheen to Dingwall and on to Inverness.

So, generally through the enterprise of local lairds and merchants in combating not only the hazards of weather, long distances and poor roads, but also the obstinacy and parsimony of the Post Office, the links with the islands were gradually forged. Typical of the difficulties which beset the Scottish postman at the close of the eighteenth century were those recounted in a memorandum submitted to the Postmaster-General for Scotland in 1798 by Lord Macdonald, General McLeod of McLeod, Ranald George Macdonald of Clanranald, and other landowners of Skye and Uist. 'The Posts from Dunvegan to Inverness, who go alternately, week about, have an allowance each of 5s. for every time they go to Inverness, a journey going and returning of fully 226 miles including six ferries. This sum of 5s., it is evident, cannot be an inducement for any man to take such a Journey, and the Post of necessity has been and is still the Carrier for the whole Country, and from being overloaded with Commissions he very frequently is detained beyond his usual time, and he generally takes a small boat at Loch Carron whereby his own life as well as the mail is in eminent danger of being lost.'

The difficulties of establishing a regular postal service between Lewis and the mainland pale into significance compared with those facing the islanders of St. Kilda when, during the 1870s, they sought to augment the occasional visits of tourist steamers by a post office of their own and a reliable mail service. One solution to their problem was the device traditionally used by shipwrecked mariners, a letter in a sealed bottle thrown into the sea. One of the first of which there appears to be definite record was launched in December 1876 and was found nine months later on the Norwegian coast. Meanwhile the survivors from an Austrian vessel wrecked off St. Kilda had prepared a more elaborate conveyance, a tiny wooden dug-out canoe which they fitted with a sail. It carried a bottle containing a letter appealing for help and it was launched on 5 February 1877. Three weeks later

8

the miniature mail-boat was found on a sandbank near Poolewe and the letter was forwarded to the Austrian consul in Glasgow. A similar letter attached to a lifebuoy had already reached Birsay, near Kirkwall, so that the ingenious sailors were soon rescued by a warship.

In 1899 the Post Office at last agreed to appoint one of the islanders to be postmaster at an annual salary of £5. The mail which he handled was delivered and collected by trawlers from Aberdeen or Fleetwood and this arrangement continued, despite complaints of irregularity, until the island was evacuated in 1930. The 'St. Kilda mail-boats', each carved from a chunk of wood with a piece of sacking for a sail, were still occasionally launched but for the benefit of visitors and Victorian philatelists rather than from postal necessity. Servicemen stationed on the island since 1957 have used new St. Kilda mail-boats from time to time as a philatelic publicity exercise but teleprinter and helicopter links with Benbecula virtually replaced the old, uncertain sea services to St. Kilda.

One advantage brought to Scotland by the Treaty of Union in 1707 was the steady increase in the prosperity of Greenock, Glasgow and the other Clyde ports, no longer handicapped by English discrimination against Scottish trade with the American colonies. The dredging and deepening of the river channel from 1770 onwards enabled larger vessels to proceed further up-river from Greenock, laying the foundations of Glasgow's overseas trade in sugar, tobacco, textiles and ship-building. As the modest cathedral and university town grew into a commercial metropolis, its great river became a highway along which the mails journeyed near and far.

The completion of the Crinan Canal in 1801 and the opening of the Caledonian Canal twenty-two years later allowed through sea traffic between Glasgow and Inverness. Henry Bell's tiny wooden paddle-steamer *Comet* ushered in a new era of transport on the West Coast when it began its passenger service from

Glasgow via Gourock to Helensburgh in 1812. Other services were developed by the Clyde Shipping Company and the Castle Company. The latter was acquired in 1851 by Glasgow and Highland Royal Mail Steamers, which was in turn acquired by one of the partners, David MacBrayne, who gave the new company his name. The red and black funnels of his steamships became so familiar and welcome a sight on the waters of the West Highlands and Islands that it was said of his Company,

> 'The Earth belongs unto the Lord
> And all that it contains;
> Except the Western Highlands,
> Which belong unto MacBrayne's'.

The Company had been carrying mails along the Clyde since 1851 and it gradually undertook most of the mail contracts for the West Highlands and Islands. Its two most celebrated steamers were the *Iona*, built in 1864, and the *Columba*, built in 1878. In July 1879 the Post Office installed travelling post offices on board these two steamers, which were running between Greenock and Ardrishaig, on Loch Fyne. Several types of postmark were used on the mail handled on board the *Iona* and the *Columba*, and later on board the *Grenadier* and *Chevalier*, which were engaged in the same service. The early postmarks were of the Duplex type with the Greenock post office number 163 between bars and, in the circular date-stamp, the words 'Greenock and Ardrishaig Packet' with the date. Later types included the ship's name, 'Iona Steamer – Greenock' or 'Iona Steamer 163' or 'Gk. & Ardrishaig Packet – Grenadier'. A check-letter 'A' in the date-stamp indicated that the letter or postcard had been posted on the outward trip made in the forenoon from Greenock, and the check-letter 'B' indicated the return trip from Ardrishaig in the afternoon. Intermediate calls were made at Gourock, Dunoon, Innellan, Rothesay, Colintraive, Tighnabruaich and Tarbert. Envelopes and postcards bearing the postmarks of the Greenock and Ardrishaig packets are keenly sought by collectors and some types are rare. The travelling post office was discontinued in April 1917 as a war economy measure.

Other Clyde steamers used rubber-stamp cachets on mail which they accepted on board for posting at Greenock. These cachets are not official postmarks, being intended simply to publicise the ship's name and its itinerary, but they are also popular with collectors. Most are to be found on picture postcards posted by tourists before the First World War. A typical example in violet ink on a picture postcard with a view of the steamer reads 'Posted on board S.S. "Fairy Queen" – Loch Eck, Argyllshire'. The postmark is 'Greenock, 7.30 p.m., JY 31, 03'. Among many other similar cachets are 'Posted on board Lord of the Isles steamer', 'Caledonian Steam Packet Co. Limited – Duchess of Montrose', and 'Glasgow and South Western Rly, Steam Vessels – P.S. Juno'.

The development of the early mail services to the Orkney and Shetland Islands followed the same pattern as other island services. Towards the end of the eighteenth century appeals from the inhabitants for regular posts were answered first by local merchants and shippers. To them, after much persuasion, the Post Office made a grant in aid, much below the cost of the service. Finally the Post Office agreed to regard letters to both destinations as 'ship letters' for which the captains of vessels carrying them were entitled to a payment of twopence per letter. This amount was charged over and above the ordinary postage. It was this system of payment to ships' captains that the Post Office used in arranging the transport of mails across the oceans of the world.

A ship letter was simply a letter which travelled part of its journey by sea. Until the introduction of uniform penny postage in 1840, the postage was normally paid by the addressee on receipt of the letter. In order that the correct amount could be calculated, Cromwell's Act of Parliament of 1657 and the 1660

Act which legalised it enjoined that any ship bringing letters to Britain must land them at the first port of call. Here the mail was accepted by the Post Office agent or postmaster, who paid the captain his fee of one penny per letter, increased by an Act of Parliament in 1799 to twopence. The letter was then stamped with a postmark bearing the name of the port and the words 'Ship Letter' before being forwarded to the General Post Office in London. A special Ship Letter Office was opened in 1799 to handle such mail. Here the postage was calculated, its three elements being the standard charge from the country of origin, the ship letter fee, and the mileage rate from the port of landing to London and thence to the final destination. There the postmaster or the letter-carrier collected the postage from the addressee.

No ship letter fee was charged on letters brought by the Post Office sailing-packets. Instead there was a packet letter fee which, as the packets were considered safer and speedier than privately owned merchant vessels, was usually double the ship letter fee. Post offices at most of the large ports in the United Kingdom had their own ship letter postmarks which included the name of the port. Some smaller ports had a postmark reading 'Ship' or 'Ship Letter' which was struck alongside the normal town postmark, and at a few ports the postmaster wrote the endorsement 'Ship Letter' in his own hand.

Letters from India, Ceylon, Mauritius, the East Indies and the Cape of Good Hope enjoyed a preferential rate of postage. In 1819 the rate was 4d for a letter weighing up to three ounces, compared with 6d per quarter-ounce for letters from other parts of the world. Because of this difference, special postmarks were needed to help the post office clerks to calculate the correct postage on such letters. These 'India Letter' postmarks are believed to have been used only at three Scottish ports, Greenock, Port Glasgow and Leith. Examples, in two lines of capital letters, are 'India Letter – Port Glasgow', 'Greenock – India Ship Lr.' and 'India Letter – Leith'.

The philatelic interest of these early letters from overseas lies in their postmarks and in the manuscript notes made on them by the clerks who handled them at various stages of their journey. The postmarks and endorsements provide evidence of the route of a letter from despatch to arrival and of the postage charged on it but the story is not always complete and the gaps in it can sometimes only be filled by the inspired guesswork which comes from a wide knowledge of postal history. The Scottish ports at which hand-stamped ship letter postmarks are known to have been used are:

| | |
|---|---|
| Aberdeen | Kirkcaldy |
| Anstruther | Kirkwall |
| Ardrossan | Leith |
| Ayr | Lerwick |
| Burntisland | Montrose |
| Campbeltown | Newburgh |
| Dumfries | Peterhead |
| Dunbar | Portaskaig |
| Dundee | Port Glasgow |
| Edinburgh | Rothesay |
| Fraserburgh | Saltcoats |
| Glasgow | Stranraer |
| Grangemouth | Thurso |
| Granton | Tobermory |
| Greenock | Troon |
| Irvine | Wick |

The designs of the postmarks vary from two straight lines of capitals giving the name of the port and words 'Ship Letter' to decorative ovals with the name, a crown and the royal cypher, G.R., of King George III. The date was seldom included in the early postmarks, as this was of no postal significance. Among the commonest markings are those of busy ports, examples being 'Ship Letter – Leith', 'Ship Letter – Greenock' and 'Ship Lre – Port Glasgow'. Other types, such as 'Portaskaig Ship', 'Pteerhd

Ship Letter' and 'Ship Letter – Burntisland', are very rare.

The introduction of uniform postage rates in the United Kingdom, 4d from 5 December 1839 and 1d from 10 January 1840, reduced the need for ship letter postmarks, as the inland postage on each letter no longer depended on the distance between the port where it was landed and its destination via London. A uniform rate of 8d per half-ounce was also introduced for each letter carried to or from the United Kingdom by private merchant vessels. Government contracts with the new steamship lines and the prepayment of postage, which could be enforced now that the rates were uniform, led to less haphazard arrangements for the carriage of overseas mail. The first contract was granted in May 1839 to a Nova Scotian ship-owner, Samuel Cunard, who founded the British and North American Royal Mail Steam Packet Company, better known as the Cunard Line, for the express purpose of running a regular steamship service between Britain and North America. His operations began on 4 July 1840 when *Britannia*, a 1,150-ton paddle-steamer built by Duncan's on the Clyde, left Liverpool with mail and passengers for Halifax and Boston. Three more Clyde-built paddle-steamers, *Acadia*, *Caledonia* and *Columbia*, quickly followed *Britannia* into service. The last trans-ocean paddle-steamer, *Scotia*, a giant of 3,850 tons, was built for Cunard by Napier's, on the Clyde, and made her final crossing in 1876.

Meanwhile control of the Post Office sailing-packets had been transferred in 1837 to the Admiralty, which had already been supervising the Falmouth packets for fourteen years. Despite the introduction of steamships, beginning at Dover in 1821 and at Portpatrick in 1825, the official services were unable to compete with those offered by the commercial steamship lines. By 1860, when it was intended that they should be returned to the control of the Post Office, the last of the mail-packets had been withdrawn from service.

The name 'packet-ship' in its French form, 'paquebot', was revived later in the century by the General Postal Union, now known as the Universal Postal Union. The purpose of this organisation, which was founded in 1874 and now embraces virtually every country in the world, was to regulate the international exchange and transport of mails, to simplify accounting procedures and to standardise rates of postage. One of the Union's first agreements covered the handling of mail transported by private merchant vessels or posted by passengers or crew on board ocean-going liners. The prepayment of postage in the country of origin was made compulsory so that, for example, American stamps would be used to prepay the postage on mail posted in an American ship on the high seas. On arrival in a British port, the mail would be handed to the local post office for postmarking, sorting and onward despatch. To indicate why American or any other foreign stamps were accepted as valid by a British postmaster, the Union agreed that special postmarks should be used on such mail. These would incorporate the words 'Ship Letter' or 'Ship Mail' but in smaller offices the ordinary date-stamp might be used provided that an additional 'Ship Letter' postmark was struck near it. In 1891 the Universal Postal Union recommended that all countries should include the French word 'Paqubot' in the postmarks used on mail of this kind.

There are many types of these maritime postmarks, some with the words 'Ship Letter' or 'Paquebot' in a straight line of capitals and others with circular hand-stamps incorporating the same words. Examples are: 'Aberdeen – Paquebot', 'Edinburgh – Paquebot', and 'Stornoway, Isle of Lewis, Paquebot.' Also used have been machine-stamped postmarks with the words 'Paquebot – Posted at sea' instead of a slogan, examples from Greenock being the commonest. Akin to the Paquebot postmarks are those used on mail landed from ships of the Royal Navy. Circular hand-stamps reading 'Edinburgh – H.M. Ships' and machine-stamped postmarks reading 'Received from H.M. Ships' or, without indication of the port of landing, 'Post Office – Maritime Mail', are frequently seen on letters posted during the two world wars.

It was these wars which interrupted and yet indirectly stimulated the development of a quicker and more flexible means of mail transport even than Samuel Cunard's ocean liners, Aberdeen trawlers or MacBrayne's steamers. The first airmail service in the United Kingdom was organised in September 1911 between Hendon airport, London, and Windsor, as part of the Coronation celebrations of King George V and Queen Mary. Proceeds from sales of the specially designed envelopes and postcards carried on the flights were devoted to compensating one of the pilots, who crashed on take-off and broke both legs, and to endowing a bed at the King Edward VII Hospital, Windsor. After the First World War, during which aircraft increased considerably in range and reliability, the introduction of regular airmail services became feasible. The pioneer flights included the spectacular attempts to fly the Atlantic, culminating in the first successful non-stop crossing by Alcock and Brown in May 1919, and the first England-to-Australia flight by the four Australians, Ross Macpherson Smith and his brother Keith, who had been educated at Wariston School, Moffat, Sergeant W. H. Shiers and Sergeant J. M. Bennett. The formation of Imperial Airways in 1924 gave added impetus to the development of overseas airmail services but within the United Kingdom the transport of mail by air was closely linked to the railway companies because of the long-established railway letter service.

The first serious attempt to run an internal air letter service was made by the Great Western Railway in April 1933, when a daily passenger service was opened between Cardiff, Teignmouth, Torquay and Plymouth. By permission of the Postmaster-General, large blue stamps showing a Westland Wessex monoplane were issued for use on the air letters. Their face value was 3d, then the postage on a railway letter. At the same time, Highland Airways Ltd., a company formed by Mr. E. E. Fresson, had started a regular passenger and freight service between Inverness and Kirkwall. The following year the company was granted a Post Office contract to carry mails and the first flight, on 29 May 1934, was commemorated by the issue of special souvenir labels priced at 2s. each and printed in red, pink and green. Inscribed 'First Airmail – Highland Airways Ltd. – Inverness – Orkney Isles – at ordinary letter rate – 29 May 1934', the labels showed a biplane against a map of the flight. Another issue of souvenir labels, priced at 1s. each, was made on 1 December 1934, when the company was granted permission to include Wick in the airmail service. Printed in pink, blue and black, these labels were inscribed 'First Airmail – Highlands Airways Ltd. – Inverness – Wick – Kirkwall – ordinary letter rate – 1st Dec. 1934'. Although not postage stamps, because they did not defray postage, these labels are now collectors' items, especially if on one of the original envelopes flown by Highland Airways.

The first British inter-city airmail service was inaugurated by Railway Air Services Ltd. on 20 August 1934 in conditions which the passengers in the two aircraft were not likely to forget. The service was scheduled to link Glasgow with Belfast. Douglas, Manchester, Birmingham and London, with connections at Birmingham for Cardiff, Teignmouth, Plymouth, Bristol, Southampton and Cowes, Isle of Wight. The aircraft left Renfrew airport in a cloudburst. Later, while crossing the Irish Sea from Belfast en route for Manchester, one aircraft ran into conditions so turbulent that Sir Harold Hartley, vice-chairman of the L.M.S. Railway and chairman of Railway Air Services, was thrown against the emergency roof exit, his head and shoulders bursting through the canvas. A Royal Air Force officer coolly stood up and held his raincoat over the puncture. When the aircraft reached Manchester, the weather was so bad that the flight to Croydon was cancelled and the mail was sent on to London by rail. Souvenir envelopes with the silhouette of a four-engined aircraft and the inscription 'Railway Air Services – First United Kingdom Air Mail by Railway Air Services Ltd.' were issued to commemorate the first flight. The route was altered in November 1934 to substitute a call at Liverpool for those at Birmingham and Manchester.

The companies which operated the early airmail services in Scotland were:

> Aberdeen Airways
> Allied Airways
> Highland Airways
> Hillman Airways
> North Eastern Airways
> Northern and Scottish Airways
> Railway Air Services
> Scottish Airways

Today the successor of those companies, British European Airways, is carrying an ever-increasing quantity of mail as part of the normal Post Office distribution within the United Kingdom. By agreement with the Post Office, B.E.A. also runs an airway letter service similar to the railway letter service. A first class letter can be handed in at certain airports and town terminals to be carried by air to the airport nearest to its destination. There it may be either called for or posted for delivery by the Post Office. Since January 1951 special stamps have been issued for use on letters carried by this service. The early designs showed the B.E.A. emblem and a map of the British Isles but three stamps issued in May 1964 featured the Hawker-Siddeley *Trident* air-liner and in May 1970 a new design showing B.E.A.'s Union Jack tail-marking was introduced.

Mail transport of the future was fore-shadowed in Scotland as long ago as July 1934, when an Austrian inventor, Gerhard Zucker, conducted experiments with small letter-carrying rockets between Harris and Scarp, in the Outer Hebrides. Labels inscribed 'Western Isles – Rocket Post' were sold at 2s 6d and 5s each to defray expenses. A cachet hand-stamped on some of the letters, 'Damaged by first explosion at Scarp, Harris', tells its own story.

**10**

## *Stamps from Overseas*

Tired of trying to keep pace with the never-ending stream of new stamp issues, most of them having little other purpose than to tempt money from collectors' pockets, many philatelists have been turning in recent years to a new type of collecting. Known as thematic or topical philately, this consists of choosing a favourite theme or topic and collecting only the stamps that illustrate it, regardless of the country from which they come. Postmarks, first day covers, souvenir envelopes and picture postcards may be used to supplement the display of stamps. Among the most popular themes are 'Ships on Stamps', 'The History of the Airmail', 'Wild Flowers', 'Music and Musicians' and 'Scouting on Stamps'. A kindred theme, particularly popular with collectors who live in a large city, is to make a study of its postal history, illustrating the collection with stamps, postmarks and picture postcards which show views of the city or portraits of its celebrities.

The collector who chooses as his theme 'Scotland on Stamps' has a wide choice of material at his disposal. As well as the British stamps described in Chapter 4, there are already dozens of issues from Commonwealth and foreign countries to illustrate the theme and new additions are constantly being made. Some, with portraits of Scots who have achieved world fame, are easy to identify but on other stamps the Scottish connection may be difficult to determine. Much of the pleasure of forming such a collection lies in the discoveries the collector may make, not only about his stamps but about Scotland, too.

Robert Burns, it has been said, is not so much a national poet as a national institution. But on the Russian stamps issued in 1956 to mark the 160th anniversary of his death he is clearly described as 'the great national poet of Scotland'. The stamps had a face value of 40-kopecks and were printed in yellow-brown by the photogravure process. The following year the same design, based on Alexander Nasmyth's portrait of the poet, was used for a second issue of 40-kopecks stamps, this time printed by the recess-engraving process with the portrait in dark brown and the frame in blue. Two years later stamps in this design were re-issued with the dates '1759-1959' added in red to mark the bicentenary of the poet's birth. Burns was also portrayed on a greenish-blue 55-bani stamp issued in Romania in 1959 as one of a series honouring foreign celebrities.

These were not the first foreign stamps to portray a poet of Scottish blood. 'Half a Scot by birth and bred a whole one' was the description applied to himself by George Gordon, Lord Byron. The son of a feckless English guards officer and of Catherine Gordon of Gight, Aberdeenshire, a descendant of the Laird of Gight who fell at Flodden, Byron spent his childhood in Aberdeen and at Ballaterach, on the Aboyne estates. There he learned that love for Scotland which is reflected in some of his best-known lines:

'England! thy beauties are tame and domestic,
To one who has rov'd on the mountains afar:
Oh! for the crags that are wild and majestic,
The steep, frowning glories of dark Loch na Garr.'

After a tempestuous life, Byron at last found the cause he could embrace whole-heartedly, the struggle of the Greeks to win their independence from Turkish rule. Elected a member of the Greek revolutionary committee, Byron landed in Greece in August 1823 to play his part in the rebellion but the following

April he died of rheumatic fever at Missolonghi. A century later, in April 1924, the Greek Post Office issued two stamps in memory of the poet's contribution to the Greek cause. One, an 80-lepta stamp in blue, showed his portrait and the other, a large 2-drachma stamp in black and violet, showed Byron among his Greek friends at Missolonghi. Another stamp with his portrait, a 5-filler magenta, was issued in Hungary in 1948 in a series honouring foreign authors and when a monument to Byron was unveiled in the Villa Borghese, Rome, in 1959, the Italian Post Office issued a special stamp to mark the occasion. It showed the statue of the poet by the Danish sculptor Bertel Thorwaldsen.

If Robert Louis Stevenson was not himself a stamp collector, there is evidence in at least one of his stories, *The Wrecker*, that he had a sound knowledge of philately. He describes an album containing 'varying shades of the English penny, Russians with the coloured heart, old undecipherable Thurn and Taxis, obsolete triangular Cape of Good Hopes, Swan Rivers with the Swan, and Guianas with the sailing ship', all readily recognisable as stamps which could well have figured in a collection formed during the 1880s. In another part of the book Stevenson makes makes one of his characters say 'When I 'eard you was a collector, I dropped all. It's a saying of mine, Mr. Dodsley, that collecting stamps makes all collectors kin. It's a bond, sir; it creates a bond.' It is in Samoa, where Stevenson spent the last years of his life, that he has been most honoured philatelically. When the first series of pictorial stamps was issued for Western Samoa in 1935, the 6d value had a view of his house, Vailima, on the island of Upolu, and the 1s stamp showed his tomb on Mount Vaea. A series issued in 1939 to mark the 25th anniversary of New Zealand control of Western Samoa included a 7d stamp with a portait of R.L.S., and when Western Samoa became an independent state on 1 January 1962, the 1s 3d stamp of the independence series showed another view of Vailima. In

1969, on the 75th anniversary of Stevenson's death, a complete series of four stamps honoured his memory. The designs featured an open book with his portrait at the left and sketches of characters from four of his books, *Treasure Island, Kidnapped, Dr. Jekyll and Mr. Hyde,* and *Weir of Hermiston,* on the right. The inscription included the name which the Samoans gave to R.L.S., 'Tustitala, Teller of Tales'.

James Barrie did not lack honours in his own lifetime. He was created a baronet in 1913, became Lord Rector of St. Andrews University in 1919, was made a member of the Order of Merit in 1922 and became Chancellor of Edinburgh University in 1930. But of all his honours, it is said, he most valued his private key to Kensington Gardens and the statue of Peter Pan which stands there. Each year the New Zealand Post Office makes a special issue of charity stamps which are sold at a small premium above their face value for postage, the extra money raised by their sale being donated to holiday camps organised for poor and ailing children. The statue of 'Peter Pan in Kensington Gardens' was featured on two stamps issued as the annual charity series in 1945.

Some of the Scots who have been honoured by issues of stamps are better known in countries overseas than they are in their own country. 'Alex MacKenzie from Canada by land, 22nd July 1793' says the laconic inscription on a rock in Dean Channel, on the Canadian Pacific coast. The inscription was reproduced on a 6-cents stamp issued in June 1970 by the Canadian Post Office to mark the 150th anniversary of the death of that Alexander Mackenzie. Born in Stornoway he emigrated as a boy to the United States, later becoming a successful fur-trader in Canada. In 1789 he began the arduous journeys of exploration which were to take him north to the Arctic Ocean, to the mouth of the great river that now bears his name, and then west to the Pacific. Here, on a rock where he and his companions had rested, he used a mixture of vermilion and melted grease to paint the rough inscription reproduced on the 1970 stamp. Mackenzie was the first European to penetrate the Rocky Mountains and to realise that British Canada might one day stretch from ocean to ocean. He was knighted in 1802 and became a member of the Lower Canada House of Assembly before returning home to end his days on the estate he purchased, Avoch House, in the Black Isle.

Canadian history, indeed, is full of Scottish names. The Earl of Selkirk, honoured by a Canadian 5-cents stamp issued in 1962, founded the Red River Settlement as a home for Scottish refugees from the Highland Clearances. As well as the Earl's portrait, the stamp shows a kilted settler sowing seed. Another emigrant to Canada at about the same period was John Alexander MacDonald, who was born in Glasgow in 1815. After a long political career during which he earned the title of 'the Disraeli of Canada', MacDonald became one of the architects of the Canadian Confederation and its first prime minister, from 1867 to 1873. His portrait has appeared on several Canadian stamps, including two in a series issued in 1927 to commemorate the sixtieth anniversary of the Confederation and another issued in 1966 to mark the centenary of the London conference at which the structure of the Confederation was planned. One of Sir John MacDonald's political opponents was another Scot, Alexander Mackenzie, who was born at Dunkeld in 1822 and emigrated to Canada as a young man, first becoming a builder and later taking office as the first Liberal prime minister of Canada. A Canadian 4-cents stamp of 1952 showed Mackenzie's portrait. Alexander Graham Bell, the Edinburgh-born inventor of the telephone, and George Brown, who was born in Alloa in 1818 and founded one of Canada's most celebrated newspapers, the Toronto *Globe*, are portrayed on other Canadian stamps.

One of the most attractive stamps ever issued in Canada is a large blue 5-cents pictorial placed on sale in August 1933 to mark the centenary of the first non-stop trans-Atlantic crossing

9

by a steamship. Shown on the stamp, the ship was the *Royal William* and although she had been built at Quebec, Scotsmen played no small part in her success. The builders were Messrs. Black and Campbell, and their foreman-designer was a young Canadian, James Goudie, who had learned his trade in Scotland. The engines were made in Montreal by Messrs. Bennet and Henderson, whose senior partner, John Bennet, had served his apprenticeship on the Clyde. The crankshaft had been forged by Robert Napier at his Govan works and the ship's master was Captain John McDougall. The *Royal William* left Pictou, Nova Scotia, on 18 August 1833 and after a rough crossing reached Gravesend twenty-five days later.

Another attractive Canadian stamp, one of a series issued at intervals in tribute to popular sports, was a 6-cents value featuring the winter game known to French-Canadians as 'le curling'. There are records of Scottish settlers curling in 1805 on the Mill Dam Pond at Beaufort, Quebec, and the Royal Montreal Curling Club, founded two years later, is the oldest in North America.

A study of the stamps of the United States, of Australia, New Zealand or southern Africa reveals as many Scottish associations as are to be found on the stamps of Canada. Alexander Graham Bell is portrayed on an American 10-cents stamp of 1940, one of a series devoted to American inventors. A series issued in 1936 to honour American naval commanders includes a 1-cent stamp portraying John Paul Jones, who was born at Kirkbean, Kircudbrightshire, in 1747 and settled in Virginia. His exploits in command of American ships during the war of independence earned him fame and recognition as one of the founders of the United States Navy. On 25 November 1960 a 4-cents stamp was issued by the American Post Office to honour another successful emigrant, Andrew Carnegie, on the 125th anniversary of his birth in Dunfermline.

Among the Scots honoured by stamps in South America are

Alexander Graham Bell, portrayed on an Argentine stamp of 1944, and Admiral Cochrane, tenth Earl of Dundonald, portrayed on stamps from Chile and Peru. Cochrane earned the gratitude of these countries for his leadership in their struggle for independence from Spanish rule. When special series were issued in Chile in 1910 and Peru in 1911 to celebrate the centenaries of their independence, a portrait of Lord Cochrane appeared in both issues.

Scottish explorers portrayed on African stamps include David Livingstone and Mungo Park. Two stamps issued in 1955 by the short-lived Federation of Rhodesia and Nyasaland marked the centenary of Livingstone's discovery of the Victoria Falls on the River Zambezi. The 3d stamp showed a view of the Falls with an aircraft above them and the 1s stamp had a portrait of the explorer with the Falls in the background. The series issued in The Gambia in September 1971 to honour Mungo Park commemorated the bicentenary of his birth at Selkirk. Two of the stamps, 25-bututs and 37-bututs, showed episodes from his African journeys and a map of the Gambia River along which he set out to explore the course of the Niger. The 4-bututs stamp had a portrait of Mungo Park with a tranquil view of Scottish hills as a background.

The celebrities portayed on Australian stamps include Sir Thomas Livingstone Mitchell, who was born at Craigend, Stirlingshire, in 1792. While Surveyor-General of New South Wales, Mitchell explored much of central Queensland and realised its potential value for pasture and grazing. As well as his portrait against a map of eastern Australia, the three stamps issued in 1946 to mark the centenary of his exploration also showed cattle and sheep to symbolise the importance of his discoveries to the development of Australian agriculture. John McDouall Stuart, born at Dysart, Fife, in 1815, was also a surveyor in Australia. He made several dangerous journeys of exploration and in July 1862 completed the crossing of the continent from south to

north. The centenary of his achievement was marked by the issue
in July 1962 of a 5d stamp with his portrait. A previous issue, a
5d stamp of 1960, had already commemorated the centenary of
Stuart's exploration of the Northern Territory. Its design reproduced a water-colour of *The Overlanders* by Sir Daryl Lindsay.
Yet another Australian surveyor, George Woodroffe Goyder,
who was born in Liverpool but educated at Glasgow High
School, was honoured by an Australian stamp issued in February 1969. This marked the centenary of the arrival of Goyder
and his party in the Northern Territory to plan the future city
of Darwin. The design showed modern buildings in Darwin and
a century-old photograph of the surveyors.

Some of the Scots on stamps are instantly recognisable. The
familiar features of King James the Sixth of Scotland and First
of England are to be seen on a stamp issued in Newfoundland in
1910 to mark the tercentenary of the charter which he granted
to John Guy, of Bristol, to establish a colony there. Both James
and his son, King Charles I, who was born in Dunfermline, are
portrayed on stamps from the West Indian island of Barbuda.
Charles has also been portrayed on stamps issued in Barbados
in 1927 to mark the tercentenary of colonisation and in 1939
for the tercentenary of the Barbados General Assembly.

Less noticeable is the Scotsman on 4-cents stamps issued in
North Borneo in 1909 and re-issued in 1916 and 1925. The
stamps show a group of men seated at a large table. In the centre
is the Sultan of Sulu and on his right is the Scotsman, an engin-
eer named William Clarke Cowie. Born in Glasgow, Cowie left
Scotland in 1865 and after trading in Singapore and the
Malayan islands, he helped to form the British North Borneo
Company. As chairman, Cowie was granted a concession by the
Sultan of Sulu – the stamp shows the negotiations in progress –
and in 1881 the Company was incorporated by royal charter.
As well as exporting timber, tobacco, rice, sago and other
tropical products, the Company governed North Borneo, a

territory the size of Ireland, until the Japanese invaded it in December 1941.

Among the most popular stamps issued in Commonwealth countries during recent years have been series featuring British soldiers in the colourful uniforms of long ago. Scottish soldiers are to be found in several of these series. An officer of a Light Company of the 93rd Regiment of Foot, the Sutherland Highlanders, in the uniform of about 1830, is shown on a stamp from Antigua and a private of the 91st Foot, the Argyllshire Highlanders, about 1832, is shown on a stamp from St. Helena. Gibraltar stamps feature an officer of the Royal Scots in the uniform of 1839 and a soldier of the Black Watch about 1845. The splendid full-dress shako of an officer of the 91st Foot, dating from about 1816, can be seen on a St. Helena stamp in a series devoted to militaria. As more countries issue stamps to illustrate the theme of 'Soldiers on Stamps', the collector will be able to find more which honour the Scottish soldier.

These brief remarks do no more than skim the surface of the subject. There is a stamp from the Malayan state of Johore portraying Mrs. Helen Wilson, of Kilmarnock, who was for a time Sultana of Johore; there is a stamp from the United States reproducing John MacWhirter's classic painting of Highland cattle, *The Vanguard;* and there is a stamp from Belgium portraying Sir Robert William Philip, the Glasgow-born physician who fought so hard to conquer tuberculosis. A stained glass window familiar to worshippers at the Church of Our Lady of Perpetual Succour, in Glasgow, is reproduced in full colour on a stamp issued in Gibraltar for use on the Christmas mails of 1970. It is for the collector to discover for himself the story behind these and the many other stamps which bring a breath of Scotland to the album.

## 11

### *Cinderella Stamps*

One of the most flourishing philatelic societies in Britain is the Cinderella Stamp Club. It was founded in 1959 by a group of London collectors, prominent among them being two of the world's leading authorities on philately, Maurice Williams and his brother L. Norman Williams, whose editorship of the Club's quarterly journal, *The Cinderella Philatelist,* has been outstandingly successful. Members of the Cinderella Stamp Club seldom glance at the usual catalogues, which list the orthodox postage stamps issued by sovereign states and recognised as legitimate by the Universal Postal Union. Instead the Club's members favour the local stamps intended for use within a limited area, fiscal and revenue stamps, telegraph stamps, bus, railway and airway letter and parcel stamps, labels publicising exhibitions and trade fairs, bogus stamps and forgeries made to deceive unwary collectors, charity and publicity stickers, Christmas seals and, in short, all the shadowy but fascinating issues which hover at the fringes of philately. These are the Cinderella stamps.

Scotland has had its fair share of such issues. In 1865 Robert Brydone, an Edinburgh printer and publisher, formed a company to undertake the delivery of unsealed circulars at a cost of one farthing each. Rowland Hill's scheme of uniform penny postage made no provision for any article to be sent by post for less than one penny. Although for a letter travelling a long distance this charge was low, Brydone, in common with other businessmen, realised that within a small and accessible area such as the city of Edinburgh a lower charge would be economically possible. After receiving legal advice that to deliver circulars and other printed matter would not infringe the Postmaster-General's long-established monopoly of letter-carrying, Brydone formed the Edinburgh and Leith Circular Delivery Company, with an office at 12 St. Andrew's Square. He issued farthing stamps in various colours showing the coat-of-arms of the city and its port, with the inscription 'Edinr & Leith Circular Delivery Company'. Stamps for parcels were similar but had the word 'parcel' instead of 'circular' and the Company's address instead of the value 'one farthing'.

The scheme was so quickly successful that a rival firm, Clark and Company, with an office at 10 Calton Street, Edinburgh, set up in opposition to Brydone and issued its own stamps showing the Company's name and address. Brydone himself extended his activities during 1866 and 1867, first to London and then to Glasgow, Aberdeen, Dundee and Liverpool. In each city stamps similar to those for the Edinburgh and Leith service were issued, their design being the appropriate city coat-of-arms. The Aberdeen, Dundee and Liverpool stamps are so rare that there has been some doubt whether any were ever genuinely used on circulars. In June 1867 Brydone and a partner, Manuel Eyre, formed the National Circular Delivery Company with the intention of providing a national network by linking the various city services. Two months later, stung by the prospect of losing so much of his most lucrative business to the new company, the Postmaster-General took legal action against a messenger of the London and Metropolitan Company for infringement of the Post Office's letter-carrying monopoly. Legal arguments centring on the claim by Brydone that a circular was not a letter were eventually resolved in June 1869 by the dismissal of his appeal to the Court of Queen's

Bench. The circular delivery companies then had to cease their activities.

By this time the stamps were attracting the attention of collectors and the companies decided to re-issue them, with additions, for sale as souvenirs. The new issues were arranged in sheets of 81, with nine rows each containing nine stamps of a different company. These were Dundee, Manchester, Glasgow, Liverpool, Aberdeen, Birmingham, London, Metropolitan (also a London company) and Edinburgh and Leith. The farthing stamps were printed in green and other values were added to the series, ½d blue, ¾d brown and 1d red. As no delivery services were ever organised by Brydone in Birmingham or Manchester, the stamps for those cities were not put into use. As well as these issues for sale to collectors, forgeries of the stamps, including bogus 2d, 3d, 4d, 6d and 9d values, also made their appearance. It is the re-issues and the forgeries, rather than the genuine original stamps, that are usually found today, even in collections formed in Victorian times. Although Robert Brydone's scheme for cheaper postage on circulars and leaflets came to an abrupt end, his enterprise prompted the Post Office to provide a similar service. On 1 October 1870 a new postage rate of one halfpenny per two ounces was introduced for inland newspapers, printed matter, samples and patterns. New reddish-brown halfpenny stamps were issued and at the same time the first British plain postcards, with a purple halfpenny stamp printed on them, were placed on sale at post offices. The postage on a postcard was increased in June 1918 to one penny but the halfpenny rate for printed matter remained unchanged, a lasting memorial to Robert Brydone's pioneer service, until May 1940.

Off the coasts of Britain there are a number of small islands, some permanently inhabited by a few people, others visited only by holiday-makers during the summer months, but for which the Post Office does not provide a collection or delivery service. The inhabitants of such islands, or their summer visitors, have the responsibility of transporting their own mail to the nearest post office on the mainland, where it can be despatched in the normal way. Arrangements are usually made with a local boat-man to perform this service and in order to pay him for his trouble it has become the practice for the inhabitants or the owners of some of the islands to issue their own postage stamps. Known to the Post Office as 'local carriage labels', these stamps may not be placed on the address side of an envelope, packet or postcard, and any item to be forwarded by the Post Office must also bear ordinary postage stamps.

There is no doubt that some of the early issues of these local carriage labels were genuinely intended as a means of defraying the cost of a local service. On the other hand there is equally no doubt that many of the labels issued during the last ten or fifteen years have been intended primarily for sale to collectors and have had face values bearing little relation to the cost of hiring a boat. It is for the collector himself to decide which of the local carriage labels issued for Scottish islands he wishes to add to his album. The wisest course is perhaps to aim at making a small representative collection of the cheaper varieties and to ignore the expensive labels or those for which there has been no evidence of correct postal use. The following are Scottish islands for which local carriage labels have been issued.

## Canna

An island in Argyll, about $3\frac{1}{2}$ miles north-west of Rum. The Laird of Canna, John Lorn Campbell, issued a 2d label in 1958, showing two shearwaters in flight. As a Post Office service was in operation to the island, the label had no postal function to perform but profits from sales have been donated to the Ship-wrecked Mariners' Society so it may be regarded as a charity seal.

## Carn Iar

One of the Summer Isles, off the coast of Wester Ross, about 16 miles north of Ullapool. Six labels, ranging from $\frac{1}{2}$d to 5s

and showing wild birds, were issued in 1960 but there is no
evidence of their having been used as local carriage labels on
mail.

## Davaar

An island at the mouth of Campbeltown Loch, Argyll, with a
lighthouse at the north-east. The first labels, 6d and 2s 6d, with
a view of the lighthouse, were issued in 1964. Since then about
200 different labels with a face value of over £10 have been
issued. To these must be added imperforate varieties of many
of the same labels and about fifty miniature sheets, usually containing one specimen of each label in the series concerned.
Subjects cover a wide range, from Churchill and Kennedy com-
memoratives to series in honour of the American Lions International Club, space exploration and the Olympic Games.

## Pabay

An island off Broadford, Skye. The first labels were issued in
1962 in values of 2½d, 3d, 9d, 1s 6d and a miniature sheet cost-
ing 2s 6d, all showing wild flowers. Since then about 200 different labels with a total face value of over £9 have been issued,
as well as imperforate varieties and miniature sheets.

## St. Kilda

A group of islands off the Outer Hebrides, now belonging to
the National Trust for Scotland. Several series of labels showing
wild birds, flowers and animals have been issued since 1968 but
these have no postal function as the Royal Air Force and later
the Army have assumed responsibility for providing the postal
services required by the personnel at the St. Kilda guided
missile range and tracking station.

## Sanda

An island off the coast of Argyll, about three miles south of
the Mull of Kintyre. Over 200 different labels have been issued

since 1962, many in similar designs to those issued for Davaar, with imperforate varieties and miniature sheets as well as the ordinary perforate labels. Most series have comprised four stamps with a face value of 3s, plus four imperforate varieties with the same face value and a miniature sheet containing two stamps with a face value of 2s 7d or 2s 9d. A complete set of a single series would therefore have a total face value of over 8s or 40p.

## Shuna

An island off the coast of Argyll, 13 miles from Oban. One issue, a mauve 2d value showing a map of the island, was made in 1949. The same labels were later re-printed in blue and over-printed 'Special Boat Run' in red for sale at £2 each to defray the cost of an extra boat trip. Only eight of these special labels are reported to have been used for the mail carried on the trip and many of the remaining labels were purchased by collectors.

## Soay

An island at the entrance to Loch Scavaig, on the south coast of Skye. About fifty labels showing wild birds and sea-shells, some with overprints in honour of Sir Winston Churchill and President John F. Kennedy, were issued between 1965 and 1967. The total face value of the ordinary labels, the imperforate varieties and the miniature sheets was about £7. In 1968 the Stamp Trade Standing Committee, established jointly by the Philatelic Traders' Society and the British Philatelic Associ-ation, reported that the labels issued for Soay could not be con-sidered as local carriage labels because the Post Office was already providing a regular service between Soay and Mallaig.

## Staffa

An island in the Inner Hebrides, 7 miles west of Mull, famous for its association with Mendelssohn's *Hebrides* (*Fingal's Cave*) *Overture*, composed after his visit to the island in 1829. Four labels, 1d, 5d, 1s 6d and 1s 9d, were issued in July 1969. Their designs featured the coat-of-arms of the island's owner, Captain Gerald Newell, a Celtic cross and a portait of Queen Victoria, a portrait of Mendelssohn with Fingal's Cave in the background, and a full-length portrait of Queen Victoria as she was when she visited the island. Another label, a 2s 6d value, showing a Sutherland Highlander, was issued in April 1970. Visitors to Staffa may post mail in Fingal's Cave and the local carriage labels are then postmarked with a circular date-stamp reading 'Posted in Fingal's Cave, Staffa' before being taken to the post office on the neighbouring island of Iona.

### Stroma

An island in the Pentland Firth, off Caithness, with a lighthouse and coastguard station. About 150 labels have been issued since 1962, although the only resident family left the island the previous year. The labels have depicted wild flowers, birds, animals and fishes but many have been re-issued with overprints in honour of Sir Winston Churchill. During 1970, for example, thirty-six overprinted labels with a total face value of over £2 were issued to mark the fifth anniversary of Churchill's death.

### Tanera More

One of the Summer Isles off the coast of Wester Ross. Six labels ranging from 1d to 2s 6d, showing fishes and a map of the islands, were issued in September 1970 to defray the cost of conveying mail to and from the post office at Achiltibuie, Garve.

Mention must also be made of the local carriage labels issued during the strike of Post Office employees which lasted from 20 January to 7 March 1971. As soon as the strike began, the Minister of Posts and Telecommunications, Mr. Christopher Chataway, M.P., abandoned the monopoly of letter-carrying which had been so jealously guarded by the Post Office for over three hundred years and announced that during the strike any private citizen or firm would be permitted to organise a mail service for the collection and delivery of letters and other articles. The only condition was that prior permission should be obtained from the head postmaster of the district in which the service was to operate. This permission does not appear to have been refused to any applicant and was, in many instances, obtained simply by telephone.

As soon as the announcement was made dozens of services were organised in all parts of the United Kingdom. Labels were hurriedly printed for use on the mail and it is clear that many of these were intended primarily for sale to collectors. Designs included portaits of Sir Rowland Hill, Sir Winston Churchill and Mr. Tom Jackson, the general secretary of the Union of Post Office Workers. The face value of the labels ranged from 1p to £1, charges being complicated by the change to decimal currency which took place during the strike, on 15 February 1971. Scottish local delivery services for which special labels were issued included the following:

Bannockburn and District Delivery Service
Clyde Post, Dumbarton
Dumfries Pony Express
Finwell Despatch Services, Ayr
G.B. Delivery, Dumfries
Glasgow Area Courier Service
Glasgow Parks Postal Service
Kelvin Penny Post, Glasgow
Paisley Penny Post

It is not always easy to distinguish between a local carriage label and a label issued to raise funds or for publicity purposes. Clearly the labels issued by bus companies such as Aberfeldy Motor Coaches, W. Alexander and Sons Ltd., Blue Band Motors Ltd., Dundee City Transport Department, Highland Omnibuses Ltd. and David MacBrayne Ltd. for use on their parcels services are well worthy of a place in a collection of Scottish

Cinderella stamps. Unfortunately the designs of these bus parcels stamps have been strictly utilitarian, so that few collectors have been attracted to them but a special society, the Great Britain Road Transport Stamp Group, has recently been formed to encourage interest in such issues.

Because of their attractive designs publicity labels or poster stamps have become very popular with Cinderella philatelists. Those produced before the First World War for exhibitions and trade fairs were usually well designed and printed but at that time they were issued in comparatively small numbers and were seldom considered, even by philatelists, as worth preserving after the event they publicised was over. Such labels are now much scarcer than many expensive postage stamps. For the Glasgow Exhibition of 1901 five labels showing a girl seated in front of a view of the exhibition site were issued. The Scottish National Exhibition held in Edinburgh in 1908 was similarly publicised by a label showing a view of the city with the coat-of-arms and a piper in the foreground. Among other early issues were five labels for the Scottish National Exhibition held in Glasgow in 1911, one for an anti-smoking exhibition in Glasgow in 1912, one for the Scottish Motor Show held in Edinburgh in 1913 and one for the Electrical Exhibition held the same year in Glasgow.

Dissatisfaction at the refusal of the Postmaster-General to issue a special postage stamp in 1959 in honour of Robert Burns prompted several Scottish organisations to issue Burns 'stamps' of their own. One, issued by the Scottish Secretariat, was priced at 'twa plack', recalling the eighteenth-century copper coin worth about a third of a penny. Printed in shades of blue, the label had a portrait of the poet and the inscription 'Now's the day and now's the hour'. A re-issue of the same label in 1964 had the additional slogan 'Free Scotland!' Another issue from the Scottish Secretariat showed a portrait of Burns, a thistle and the Scottish flag, with the oft-quoted lines from his ode *To a*

*Mouse,* 'The best laid schemes o' mice and men gang aft agley, and leave us naught but grief and pain for promised joy'. More recent labels from the Scottish National Party have honoured Burns, William Wallace, St. Andrew and the Declaration of Arbroath. In April 1967 the Royal Bank of Scotland gained a lot of publicity for its savings scheme by placing on sale attractive halfcrown stamps with a profile portrait of David Dale (1739-1806), the Bank's first joint agent in Glasgow. These savings stamps were replaced in 1971 by 10p and 50p stamps featuring the Bank's insignia. None of these issues have any postal validity but they make an interesting and colourful display in a collection devoted to the Scottish theme.

Eventually, as a study of English literature will confirm, Cinderella was able to go to the ball, where despite her neglect of the licensing hours and her carelessness with footwear she found a handsome Prince and happiness ever after. Occasionally, too, a Cinderella stamp finds itself similarly courted by collectors and becomes the philatelic equivalent of the belle of the ball, a stamp with an album page all to itself. One of these Cinderellas has many Scottish associations.

In November 1845 a notice appeared in a Trinidad newspaper, the *Port of Spain Gazette.* Headed 'Steamer Lady McLeod', it continued 'Letters, Money and Small Parcels will be carried from this date for subscribers only at one dollar per month from each Subscriber or Estate, payable quarterly in advance; letters of non-subscribers will be charged ten cents each. Letter Box at Michael Maxwell's, San Fernando, and Turnbull, Stewart and Co., Port of Spain. N.B. The Commander can only be held responsible for parcels or letters containing money, for which a receipt is given and a commission paid of one-half per cent. Turnbull, Stewart and Co., Marine Square, 21st Nov., 1845.'

The *Lady McLeod* was a sixty-ton steam-and-sail vessel built in 1845 by Napier's on the Clyde. She was owned by the Trinidad firm of Turnbull, Stewart and Company, and was named after Lady McLeod, wife of Sir Henry McLeod, the governor of Trinidad. Her first voyage between Port of Spain and San Fernando had been made a few weeks before the notice appeared in the *Gazette*. A year later the ship was sold to another proprietor, David Bryce. As the amount of mail being carried by the steamer was steadily increasing, the new owner found difficulty in securing payment of the postage on the letters sent by non-subscribers. In April 1847 a notice in the *Port of Spain Gazette* revealed the method by which he proposed to overcome the difficulty. 'The Subscriber experiencing inconvenience in collecting the Money for Letters of Non-Subscribers, has procured Labels, which may be had of him or the Agents for the Steamer, at five cents each, or Four Dollars per Hundred. No other Letters but those of subscribers who have paid in advance, or such as have these labels attached, will be carried, from and after the 24th instant. Freight for parcels and small packages as heretofore. (Signed) David Bryce, Proprietor.'

These labels were the first adhesive postage stamps to be issued in a British colony but they were a strictly local issue valid for use only on letters carried by the private steamer service between the two Trinidad ports. Lithographed in dark blue, they showed a spirited picture of the *Lady McLeod* at speed, smoke belching from her funnel, and a monogram comprising the initials of her name, L Mc L. There is no record of the precise period when the stamps were in use but in December 1849 David Bryce sold his ship to another Trinidad firm. Collectors do not seem to have become aware of the existence of the stamps for nearly twenty years and even then they were considered either completely bogus or a private issue of no philatelic interest. In 1867 the *Stamp Collector's Magazine* mentioned one specimen, adding scornfully 'The possessor asked the modest sum of FIVE GUINEAS for this copy which, if genuine, half a crown ought to more than buy'. A few years later *The Philatelical Journal,* which often gave news of local stamps, printed a detailed reference list of Trinidad issues beginning with those of 1851 and making no mention whatever of the *Lady McLeod* stamp.

The fairy godmother appeared in the shape of the editor of the Stanley Gibbons catalogue. He decided that the stamp was of sufficient interest to include in his list of Trinidad issues in the 1917 edition of the catalogue of British and Colonial stamps. Until then specimens had been changing hands at less than £15 each but during the last fifty years they have risen steadily in price. A collector would now expect to pay as much as £1,000 for a mint specimen in first class condition and about £400 for one with an ink cross or a corner torn off, showing that it had been used on a letter carried by the little Clyde-built steamer with the good Hebridean name.

10

## *Sources and Societies*

There were stamp collectors and dealers almost as soon as there were postage stamps. In 1856 a Plymouth youth started selling foreign stamps from a corner of the family chemist's shop. His name was Stanley Gibbons and the firm he founded is still recognised as one of the world's foremost philatelic dealers. In a 20-page price-list published in November 1865, Stanley Gibbons offered used Penny Blacks at a penny each or sixpence a dozen. The latest Stanley Gibbons catalogue, a 'simplified' edition which does not include minor varieties of colour, perforation or watermark, runs to about 2,000 pages and used Penny Blacks are listed at £9 each.

The first catalogue of stamps was compiled by a French printer, Oscar Berger-Levrault, and published in Strasbourg in September 1861. At about the same time another French collector, Alfred Potiquet, compiled a more detailed 44-page catalogue which was published in Paris. The first catalogue in English, entitled *Aids to Stamp Collectors*, was compiled by Frederick W. Booty and published in Brighton in April 1862. One of the earliest philatelic handbooks was *Forged Stamps: How to Detect Them*, written by a Birmingham dealer, Edward Loines Pemberton, and Thornton Lewes, who was at Edinburgh High School. The book was published in 1863 by Colston and Son, of 80 Rose Street, Edinburgh, at one shilling.

By this time many dealers in stamps were advertising in boys' magazines and the first philatelic journals were making their appearance. They were the *Monthly Intelligencer,* which was published in Birmingham in September 1862 and catered for several hobbies as well as philately, and the *Monthly Advertiser,* later known as the *Stamp Collectors' Review,* which began publication in Liverpool in December 1862 and was devoted entirely to philately. Even the serious lay Press was beginning to take note of the new hobby. 'The Stamp Mania' was the title of an article which appeared in *Chambers's Journal* for 6 June 1863, and *Blackwood's Magazine* had 'A Hint to Postage Stamp Collectors' in its January 1865 issue. Scottish dealers seem to have been centred in Glasgow, about twenty of them having advertised in the *Boy's Own Magazine* and other periodicals during 1863, compared with only two from Edinburgh and one from Falkirk.

One of the first philatelists to make a methodical collection of early philatelic literature was James Ludovic Lindsay, Earl of Crawford and Balcarres. The nucleus of his collection was provided by the library of an American collector, John Kerr Tiffany, which the Earl bought in 1901 for $10,000, but he added considerably to this so that when he died in 1913 he was able to leave more than 4,000 volumes to the British Museum. Another notable philatelic bibliophile was Mr. P. J. Anderson, librarian of the University of Aberdeen, who had begun collecting stamps as a boy at the Royal Academy, Inverness. At a meeting of the Aberdeen and North of Scotland Philatelic Society held in the library of Marischal College on 11 October 1911, Mr. Anderson displayed about two hundred early books and stamp albums, and recalled that his own first contribution to the literature of philately had been an article on the subject of 'Permanent Stamp Albums' in the *Stamp Collector's Magazine* for April 1869.

Today the British philatelic Press is the most versatile and informative in the world and the wise collector subscribes to at least one or two of the wide range of periodicals which are available. The following are the principal journals:

SCOTTISH PHILATELY ONLY

*Scottish Stamp News* (Pub. The Alba Stamp Group, 34 Gray Street, Glasgow G3 7TY) monthly, free to members.

UNITED KINGDOM PHILATELY ONLY

*Post Office Philatelic Bulletin* (pub. Post Office Philatelic Bureau, Waterloo Place, Edinburgh EH1 1AB) monthly, by yearly subscription.

*The Philatelic Journal of Great Britain* (pub. Robson Lowe Ltd., 50 Pall Mall, London, SW1Y 5JZ) quarterly.

WORLD PHILATELY

*Philatelic Magazine* (pub. Harris Publications Ltd., 42 Maiden Lane, London, WC2E 7LW) monthly.

*Philatelist and Postal Historian* (pub. Robson Lowe Ltd., 50 Pall Mall, London, SW1Y 5JZ) monthly.

*Philately* (pub. The British Philatelic Association, 446 Strand, London, WC2R ORA) quarterly.

*Stamp Collecting* (pub. Stamp Collecting Ltd., 42 Maiden Lane, London, WC2 7LL) weekly.

*Stamp Magazine* (pub. Link House Publications Ltd., Link House, Dingwall Avenue, Croydon, CR9 2TA) monthly.

*Stamp Monthly* (pub. Stanley Gibbons Magazines Ltd., Drury House, Russell Street, London, WC2B 5HD) monthly.

One of the difficulties facing the collector of Scottish stamps, postmarks and items of postal history is that there are so few books to help him in his researches. The most useful general catalogue of postage stamps is *Stamps of the World,* published by Stanley Gibbons Ltd., London. This gives lists of almost 160,000 stamps, with details of their designs, colours, date of issue and the retail prices charged by Stanley Gibbons Ltd. for specimens in mint and used condition. The catalogue is popularly known as the 'Simplified' because it does not include minor varieties of colour, perforation or watermark. Such varieties, which are not usually of interest to the thematic collector, are to be found in other Stanley Gibbons catalogues. The only comprehensive and authoritative survey of Scottish postal history is *Three Centuries of Scottish Posts: an Historical Survey to 1836*, by A. R. B. Haldane, published by the University Press, Edinburgh, in 1971. Since this stops short at 1836, it does not deal with postage stamps and it makes only a passing mention of postmarks but it would be of considerable help to a collector making a study of the postal history of a Scottish town or county. Other books containing some Scottish material are:

*Britain's Post Office* by Howard Robinson (Oxford University Press, 1953)

*The Penny Post, 1680-1918* by Frank Staff (Lutterworth Press, 1964)

*Carrying British Mails Overseas* by Howard Robinson (George Allen and Unwin, 1964)

*The Royal Mail: its Curiosities and Romance* by James Wilson Hyde (William Blackwood and Sons, 1884)

*James Chalmers, Inventor of the Adhesive Postage Stamp* by W. J. Smith and J. E. Metcalfe (David Winter and Son Ltd., 1970)

*British Post Office Numbers, 1844-1906* by G. Brumell (R. C. Alcock Ltd., 1968)

*Not Proven* by John Gray Wilson (Secker and Warburg, 1960) (The story of the trial of Madeleine Smith)

*Twelve Years of Scottish Air Mails* by N. C. Baldwin (Francis J. Field Ltd., 1947)

*Discovering Picture Postcards* by C. W. Hill (Shire Publications Ltd., 1970)

*The Post Office* by Sir Evelyn Murray (G. P. Putnam's Sons Ltd., 1927)

*Cinderella Stamps* by L. N. and M. Williams (William Heinemann Ltd., 1970)

*Farthing Delivery: a Fight for Cheaper Postage* by Donald S. Patton (Lowe and Brydone (Printers) Ltd., 1960)

*Catalogue of British Local Stamps* compiled by Gerald Rosen (B.L.S.C. Publishing Co., 1971)

For collectors of British stamps and postal stationery newly placed on sale, the Post Office Philatelic Bureau in Edinburgh provides a reliable service, offering mint stamps, presentation packs of new issues, first day covers and other philatelic material at cost plus a small handling charge. Full details of the Bureau's service may be obtained from the Manager, Post Office Philatelic Bureau, Waterloo Place, Edinburgh EH1 1AB.

Almost every sizeable town and city in the United Kingdom has its own philatelic society. Meetings are usually held fortnightly or monthly and subscriptions are nominal, the most usual being 50p per year for junior collectors and £1 for adults. Among the activities organised by most societies are illustrated lectures by visiting experts, short displays by members, exchange nights, auction sales, quizzes and competitions. The name and address of one's nearest society can usually be obtained from the local public library but in case of difficulty the editor of any philatelic journal will supply the information to anyone sending a stamped envelope for his reply.

The following list of the best known Scottish societies includes the name and address of the honorary secretary, to whom enquiries regarding membership may be made:

*Aberdeen and North of Scotland Philatelic Society* (1910) Bruce Walker, 21 Orchard Street, Aberdeen AB2 3DA.

*Alba Stamp Group* Stanley K. Hunter, 34 Gray Street, Glasgow G3 7TY.

*Arbroath Philatelic Society* D. Wyllie, 1 Addison Place, Arbroath.

*Ayrshire Philatelic Society* (1938) Robert I. Hislop, Carradale, 191 Whitletts Road, Ayr.

*Bearsden Philatelic Society* (1946) E. N. Morris, 76 Switchback Road, Bearsden, Glasgow G61 1AF.

*Border Philatelic Society* Miss S. Williams, 6 Island Street, Galashiels, Selkirkshire.

*Caledonian Philatelic Society* Miss M. G. Wilson, 30 Viewfield, Airdrie ML6 9DL.

*Dundee Philatelic Society* (1905) R. S. I. Goodfellow, 56 Balgillo Road, Broughty Ferry, Dundee.

*Dunfermline Philatelic Society* (1946) J. D. Inglis, 14 Whirlbut Street, Dunfermline.

*Edinburgh Philatelic Society* (1927) Arthur Walker, 41 Ross Gardens, Edinburgh EH9 3BR.

*Falkirk Philatelic Society* A. H. Brown, 25 West Bridge Street, Falkirk.

*Glasgow Philatelic Society* (1920) S. R. Mackenzie, Creag an Fhithich, Fetlar Road, Bridge of Weir, Renfrewshire.

*Glasgow Police Force Philatelic Society* George MacKenzie, 44 Brenfield Avenue, Glasgow G44 3LR.

*Glasgow Thematic Society* H. Anderson, 54 Maxwell Drive, East Kilbride.

*Harland Philatelic Society,* J. Fernie, 9 Dunmar Crescent, Alloa.

*Kirkcaldy Philatelic Society* D. Horlock, 19 Burnside Avenue, Kinghorn, Fife.

*Kircudbright Philatelic Society* Mrs. M. I. McKeand, Sulwath, Tongland Road, Kircudbright.

*Kirkintilloch Philatelic Society* James Leitch, 22 Kirkintilloch Road, Lenzie, Kirkintilloch, Glasgow G66 4RL.

*Lanarkshire Philatelic Society* (1967) James Davidson, The Schoolhouse, Auldhouse, East Kilbride.

*Moray Philatelic Society* (1950) Mrs. C. Snedden, Dalvey Lodge, Forres.

*Paisley Philatelic Society* William Martin, 4b Cedar Place, Barrhead, Glasgow.

*Perth Philatelic Society* (1961) D. N. Mackay, 8 Linton Terrace, Burghmuir, Perth.

*St. Andrews Philatelic Society* (1946) Charles K. Karsten, 32 Warrack Street, St. Andrews.

*Scottish Philatelic Society* (1890) N. M. Hay, 19 Greenhill Place, Edinburgh 10.

*Solway Philatelic Society* E. L. Whitehead, 34 Oaklands, Chapel Cross, Annan.

*Stirling Philatelic Society* (1936) J. S. Merrylees, 5 Williamfield Avenue, Stirling.

*J. P. Coats Philatelic Society* (membership restricted to employ-ees of Messrs. J. P. Coats Ltd., but visitors welcomed) Miss J. Henderson, 51 Carbeth Road, Milngavie, Glasgow.

In addition there are a number of specialist societies intended for collectors interested in the stamps and postal history of a particular country or group of countries. These societies con-duct most of their activities by post, usually publishing a journal or news-letter to which members contribute accounts of their researches. Most societies run sales or exchange packets by which members can purchase new material and sell their duplicates. Membership of one of these societies may bring the collector into contact, at least by correspondence, with collec-tors of similar interests in the United Kingdom or overseas. Among the societies catering particularly, but not exclusively, for collectors of British stamps and postmarks, and therefore for those of Scotland, the following are the best known:

*The British Philatelic Association* (1926) 446 Strand, London, WC2R ORA.

*British Postmark Society* (1958) Hon. Sec. George R. Pearson, 42 Corrance Road, London, S.W.5.

*Great Britain Philatelic Society* (1955) Hon. Sec. P. J. D'Arcy, 67 Cissbury Ring South, London, N.12.

*The National Philatelic Society* (formerly *The Junior Philatelic Society*) (1899) 44 Fleet Street, London, E.C.4.

*The Postal History Society* (1936) Hon. Sec. W. R. Wellsted, Colesgrove Manor, Goff's Oak, Waltham Cross, Herts.

*The Society of Postal Historians* Hon. Sec. V. D. Vandervelde, 25 Sinclair Grove, London, N.W.11.

*Cinderella Stamp Club* (1959) Hon. Sec. H. E. Tester, 373 Whitton Dene, Isleworth, Middlesex.

*Raflet Stamp Club* (intended for past and serving members of the Royal Air Force) Hon. Sec. A. G. Groom, 6 Grove Court, Falkland Grove, Dorking, Surrey, RH4 3DL.

*Scout Stamps Collectors' Club* (for collectors of stamps connected with the Scout Movement) Scottish Section: Hon. Sec. Stanley K. Hunter, 34 Gray Street, Glasgow G3 7TY.

A useful forum for the discussion of matters concerning the hobby of philately is provided by the Scottish Philatelic Congress. Now arranged by the Association of Scottish Philatelic Societies, formed in 1946, the Congress meets annually as the guest of one of the Scottish philatelic societies, its council consisting of one member from each society. Lectures, displays, discussions and an exhibition are staged in connection with the meetings of Congress, as well as awards to prominent philatelists. The Association's honorary secretary is Mr. J. Miller McGrath, 11 Auchenbaird, Sauchie, Alloa, Clackmannanshire.

The Scottish Philatelic Congress has its counterpart in England, the Philatelic Congress of Great Britain, which first met in Manchester in 1909. It now meets annually, usually in England, though the 1913 Congress was held in Edinburgh and that of 1924 in Glasgow. For both meetings in Scotland publicity labels were issued, those for Edinburgh showing the Scott Monument in Princes Street and those for Glasgow showing the city coat-of-arms. The honorary secretary of the Philatelic Congress of Great Britain is Mr. E. F. Hugen, 3 The Woodlands, London Road, Brighton.

Among philatelic events in Scotland during recent years have been several notable exhibitions. One, entitled *Scotex*, was organised in Glasgow in April 1962 by the Association of Scottish Philatelic Societies. As a souvenir of the event a large postcard showing, in full colour, eleven Victorian and Edwardian stamps bearing typically Scottish postmarks was placed on sale. In April 1965 the Scottish Philatelic Society celebrated its diamond jubilee with a conference and exhibition at Bridge of Allan. A three-day national exhibition, *Scophilex*, was held in Glasgow in April 1970, among the exhibits being some of the original letters and envelopes produced in evidence at the trial of Madeleine Smith. Such exhibitions are usually commemorated by specially designed postmarks which are used on mail posted at the temporary post office attached to the exhibition. A visit to a philatelic congress or exhibition is a rewarding experience. It provides the collector with opportunity to see how others display their treasures, to appreciate the results of others' researches, and to make contact with that wide fraternity of people of all ages and walks of life who are devotees of philately in general and of Scottish philately in particular.

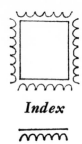

# Index